THE ULTIMATE GUIDE TO

# Getting Hired in College Sports

THIRD EDITION

Howard Gauthier, Ph.D.

Sport Leadership Publishing Company
Meridian, Idaho

THE ULTIMATE GUIDE TO

# Getting Hired in College Sports

Published by:

Sports Leadership Publishing Company
P.O. Box 792
Meridian, ID  83680-0792
www.sportsleadershippublishing.com

Sports Leadership Publishing Company is a Division of Sports Careers Institute, LLC

ISBN:  978-0-9798647-5-9

Library of Congress Control Number:  2018900214

# Contents

# Introduction

The third edition of *Getting Hired in College Sports* presents the latest strategies and techniques for conducting a successful and efficient job search in the sports world. It is a culmination of the latest research on the topic and includes the many experiences I've gained during my 30+ years in college coaching and administration.

*Getting Hired in College Sports* is designed as a resource guide for job seekers at every stage of the job search process. Therefore, most people will not read the book from cover-to-cover; rather they will turn to the section that applies to their current situation within the job search process. The exception would be for someone who is just entering the profession and is learning the in's and out's of the college sports industry.

## Where Should I Begin

Each stage within the job search process is vitally important. However, depending upon your situation, you should identify which stage of the job search process is the most appropriate place for you to begin. For example, if you already know what type of position you want for your next job, you might be able to skip the Self-Assessment Stage. However, it is recommended that you still conduct the self-assessments because they apply to every aspect of the job search process. These assessments will help you to know what skills and traits you possess, so you can use this information in your sales pitch, while answering interview questions, and during your follow-up after the interview. To determine where you should begin in the job search process, identify which of the four statements below best describe your current situation. Then refer to the paragraph that follows these statements to see where your main focus should be.

1. I feel as if I am lost. I am not sure what type of job or career I want.

2. I think I know what type of job I want, but is there a type of job that I am better suited for?

3. I know what type of position is right for me, but I cannot get an interview.

4. I am getting interviews, but I cannot land the job.

If you answered #1 or #2, you need to initially focus on the testing and assessments sections of the job search process. Once you have completed these sections, you now will turn your attention to the search stage. If you answered #3, your greatest focus needs to be on preparing for your job search. Finally, if you answered #4, you need to review the information regarding interviewing skills and follow-up strategies. You will also want to look into expanding into different target markets.

<u>Organizing Your Search</u>

Within the job search process there are 10 sections that you will be introduced to within *Getting Hired in College Sports*. These 10 sections will include the following topics:

Section 1: *Assessments*

Section 2: *Career Planning Guide*

Section 3: *Target Market*

Section 4: *Promotional Materials*

Section 5: *Sales Pitch*

Section 6: *Interview Preparation Form*

Section 7: *Interview Questions*

Section 8: *Promotional Campaign*

Section 9: *Interviewing Basics*

Section 10: *Strategic Follow-up*

To help you with your organization, you will want to create a personal job search binder that keeps each of these sections, and all of this information, organized and readily available. Best of luck in your job search and God Bless!

CHAPTER 1

# Types of Jobs in College Sports

orking in college sports can be very exciting and rewarding. Envision for a moment that you were the event manager under the bright lights of the 2018 national football championship game in Atlanta between Georgia vs Alabama. In a knock-down, drag-out game, Alabama battled back from a 13-point deficit and scored a touchdown with 3:56 remaining to tie the game at 20-20. A strong defensive stance by the Crimson Tide, a punt by Georgia, and a missed field goal with no time remaining . . . and the game is sent to overtime. On the first possession in overtime Georgia kicked a 51-yard field goal to take the lead, but Alabama wasn't to be denied as they connected on a 41-yard pass play for a touchdown and the national championship.

Not only was this a great game for the fans to watch, and the participants to play, but it was exciting for you as well. See, as the events manager, you were responsible for staging the game. Or maybe you were the official scorer of the Sweet 16 basketball game when Florida and Wisconsin played one of the greatest games ever. Wisconsin stormed back from a 12-point deficit with just over 4 minutes remaining and hit a three pointer with only

2.1 seconds remaining to send the game into overtime. The Badgers did it again when they hit two free throws with only four seconds remaining in overtime to take a two-point lead. But, like Alabama in the national championship football game, Florida wasn't to be denied in basketball. They hit an unbelievable three-point shot as time expired. The officials came to you as the official scorer to watch the monitor, to make sure the shot was a 3-pointer, and that it was shot before the clock expired. Sure enough, Florida wins and advances to the Elite Eight. You were in the middle of this excitement.

For many, these scenarios are a dream come true. For you, this is your job. The excitement is real; you are living a dream. But it doesn't have to be a bowl game or in the NCAA tournament. It can be the University of Western Montana or the College of Southern Idaho; it can be St. Thomas University or the University of Nebraska-Kearney. The excitement is still there. You are still an integral part of the game. But the game is much more than the final score. College sports are about the development of students, about the enhancement of student life, about creating community pride, and about the business of sports.

Jobs in college sports primarily fall into three main categories – coaching, administration, and positions within affiliated organizations. This chapter provides an in-depth look into the various types of jobs that are associated with these three professions. The remaining chapters help to prepare you with the strategies and organization for a focused and effective job search campaign.

## Coaching

There are five main types of coaching positions within a college athletic department: head coaches, assistant coaches, graduate assistants, strength and conditioning coaches, and various administrators (i.e. director of operations, analysts, etc.). Depending upon the level of the sports program, both head coaches and assistant coaches can be employed in one of three capacities – as a full-time position that only includes coaching duties, as a full-time position that also includes additional duties within the college (e.g. teaching, administration, etc.), or as a part-time position. The director of operations, video coordinator, and administrative analysts are typically associated with an NCAA Division I program and is an administrative position within the sports program.

## Head Coach

Head coaches may or may not be employed full-time on campus. Quite often, when a coach is employed full-time on campus, they have other duties assigned to them in addition to their coaching duties. This of course is largely dependent upon the sport and the level of competition. For example, a golf coach at a small college may or may not be a full-time on-campus employee, whereas, a basketball or football coach at the NCAA Division I level is definitely a full-time position that only includes coaching related duties.

The coach who is assigned additional duties within their contract usually will either teach on-campus or will have other administrative duties within the athletic department. Teaching duties are typically in the area of health, wellness, or physical education. This of course is dependent upon the qualifications of the person and the needs of the institution. Additional administrative duties that a coach can be assigned can quite often include one or more of the following areas: game management, marketing, fund raising, compliance, equipment management, facilities management, or intramurals.

A college head coach is responsible for developing and managing the entire program for their sport. This includes recruiting players, providing leadership for the team, assuring academic success of their student-athletes, planning practices, skill instruction, scouting opponents, preparing for contests, adhering to rules compliance, managing the budget, fundraising, and being a good colleague within the department.

## Assistant Coach

Like the head coach, an assistant coach can have a wide variety of duties. These positions differ, however, in that there are many more types of assistant coaches. Assistant coaches can range from being a full-time coaching-only position, to full-time on-campus with other duties, to part-time coaching duties, to a graduate assistant coach, and finally to a volunteer assistant coach. The titles of an assistant coach can also vary from associate head coach, to assistant coach, to a position coach (i.e. offensive coordinator or running backs coach), to a graduate assistant, to a strength and conditioning coach, to a chief administrator, or even a video coordinator.

The higher the level of competition, the more specialized the positions. For example, a top-level NCAA Division I football program will have 10 full-time assistant coaches who are responsible for recruiting, scouting, and skill instruction. By contrast, an NCAA Division II program or an NAIA program might have significantly fewer assistant coaches. These coaches may or may not be employed as full-time coaches, and it is possible that he or she is a graduate assistant. Finally, at the other end of the spectrum is an assistant coach at a small college such as an NCAA Division III program or a junior college program. He or she might be a volunteer assistant coach or receive a very small stipend. This of course varies by institution and is typically in alignment with the needs and philosophy of the college.

## Director of Operations

Many college sports programs are limited to the number of assistant coaches they can employ. To allow the head coach and assistant coaches to be more involved with skills instruction and the activities of coaching, the NCAA has allowed these programs to hire a director of operations. The director of operations has sport-specific administrative responsibilities and therefore they do not count in the institution's coaching limitation. Since a director of operations is an administrative position, they are not permitted to be involved in instructional activities or on-court/field activities with the student-athletes.[1]

The actual duties that the operations person performs are very program specific. These activities can include on-campus recruiting, management of camps/clinics, videotape exchange, travel arrangements, budgeting, tracking the academic progress of the student-athletes, and charting of statistics. The actual duties performed will differ from program to program. An example of the duties that a director of operations is involved in is seen at California State University-Bakersfield where the Director of Operations within the women's basketball program is responsible for five main areas: student managers, video filming and editing, locker room management, gear management, and special duties as assigned by the head coach. The director of operations also assists with camps, budgets, schedules, scouting, team travel, and more.[2] It is because of these wide-array of duties that quite often makes the position of director of operations a stepping-stone for breaking into the college coaching ranks.

## Administration

In comparison to coaching, administration within college sports is much broader in nature. There are several different types of positions both within intercollegiate athletics and recreational sports.

Intercollegiate athletics are programs where individuals or teams from one college or university compete in a sport against students from another college or university. In order to support these student-athletes, a variety of positions exist such as an athletic director who is responsible for the oversight of the entire department.

Other specialized positions within a college athletic department can include: an associate or assistant athletic director, a senior woman administrator, a compliance officer, academic support personnel, a business manager, game management, equipment management, marketing, fundraising, and sports information. At the highest level of competition is a full-time person, or groups of people, that typically perform these duties. However, at a lower level of competition, an athletic department might only have one or two staff members – the athletic director and possibly his or her assistant. In this situation, the administrators would be responsible for performing all of the administrative duties within the athletic department.

In recreational sports, there are several types of administrative and support positions that help to organize and stage recreational activities. Recreational sports are programs where students are active in sporting activities such as biking, kayaking, rock climbing, and swimming. Additional recreational activities are formed through intramural sports and club sports. Intramural sports are activities where students compete against other students on the same campus, whereas club sports are activities where students compete against off-campus competition such as community sport teams and club teams from other colleges. The number of club sports a college or university has is typically correlated to the size of their student enrollment. For example, according to the University Oregon's website, in the Fall Term of 2017, UO had 42 club sports ranging from cycling and disc golf to ice hockey and volleyball.[3]

As with club sports, typically a major college or university will also have a large offering of recreational programs. Therefore, these major universities will also have a large staff. For example, the staff directory for the Campus Recreation Department at the University Arizona shows that the department has 32 staff members.[4] In contrast, a small to medium size college might merge the duties of the intramural director with those of a coach. This is seen at Wheaton College where the head cross country and track coach is also the intramural director, and the head softball coach oversees the club sports program.[5]

Regardless of the size of the college or university, most college campuses have recreational sports and activities at some level.

As such, these institutions all need people to perform the duties associated with these recreational activities.

## Affiliated Associations and Organizations

In addition to coaching and administration, there are many individuals, groups, and associations that service the programs within college sports. Conferences, leagues, national associations, and sports associations typically govern and support the coaches, administrators and/or the athletic departments that are members within these associations. Each of these organizations have staff positions.

Every intercollegiate sport has a coaches' association and so does each administrative area. For example, the association for athletic directors is the National Association of Collegiate Directors of Athletics (NACDA). The governing association for men's basketball is the National Association of Basketball Coaches (NABC), and for recreation and intramural sports the association is the National Intramural-Recreational Sports Association (NIRSA). For teaching physical education or sports management the professional organization is the American Alliance for Health, Physical Education, Recreation, and Dance (AAHPERD, now known as SHAPE America). Finally, an association specifically for teaching sports administration is the North American Society for Sports Management (NASSM).

There are at least seven national governing associations within intercollegiate athletics: The National Collegiate Athletics Association (NCAA), The National Association of Intercollegiate Athletics (NAIA), The National Junior College Athletic Association (NJCAA), The National Christian College Athletic Association (NCCAA), the United States Collegiate Athletic Association (USCAA), U Sports (the Canadian universities sport association), and Canadian Collegiate Athletic Association (CCAA).

Each of these national associations have employees who serve the college athletic programs they govern. The NCAA, for example, has many employees who cover a variety of duties. These include positions that service their membership, conduct championships, monitor rules compliance, promote the organization, along with a variety of other types of positions. As you can probably tell, the NCAA is a very large organization and they have a very large work force.

Conference offices are also a good employment option. Again, depending upon the size of the conference and the level of competition, a conference may have one or more of the following – a commissioner, a chief of staff, compliance officer, director of media relations, director of championships, and a director of marketing.

In 2018, there were 35 conferences that participated in the NCAA Division I, 25 conferences in the NCAA Division II, and 45 in the NCAA Division III.[6]  In addition, the NAIA had 21 conferences[7], the NJCAA had over 520 schools in 25 regions[8], the California Community College system had 107 schools[9], and the Pacific Northwest had 36 schools that are serviced by the NWAACC.[10]  While NCAA Division I and NCAA Division II conferences have several staff members, the smaller conferences typically have limited staffs.  In some cases, these smaller conferences may only have a part-time commissioner.

Other types of organizations that are associated with college sports include all of the coaches' associations, each of the professional associations, the associations aligned with recreational sports, and the many products that are sold every day to sports programs within the various colleges and universities.  These products include a wide variety of sporting goods such as shoes, balls, uniforms, scoreboards, bleachers, promotional items, and exercise equipment.  The list goes on and on.  In essence, there are thousands of jobs in and associated with college sports.  The key is to identify what type of job you want, what the qualifications are, get those qualifications, and begin your career search campaign for the type of job and career that you are seeking.

The following is a list that outlines the various types of positions that exist within a college athletics department. It is followed by a list of the types of positions that exist within recreational sports.

## Positions in a College Athletic Department

**Director of Athletics** (Another title can include Vice-President for Athletics)– An athletic director is considered the top executive in the athletic department. They are responsible for leading and managing the entire department, including the planning, budgeting, developing, and directing all of athletic programs. They are also responsible for hiring coaches, scheduling competition, building or repairing facilities, marketing of the department and its programs, working closely with boosters (fund raising), and ensuring compliance with all of the governing authorities. The position requires an individual who is an effective and articulate leader who will represent the athletics department on campus, in the community, and within the conference. **Experience:** A college degree is required and a master's degree is preferred. The degree should be in the area of business administration or sports administration. Previous administrative or managerial experience is necessary, and previous coaching experience is preferred.

**Senior Woman Administrator** – The Senior Woman Administrator (SWA) is the highest-ranking female administrator in the athletic department. She reports directly to the athletic director. Her duties will vary depending on the need of the department. Quite often the areas of responsibility can include overseeing the operations of the department, supervising coaches, compliance, academic affairs, fiscal affairs, coaching a sport, or a combination of these. **Experience:** A college degree is required and a master's degree is preferred. Previous experience in college athletics is necessary.

**Associate/Assistant Athletic Director** (Other titles can include Senior Associate Athletic Director, Deputy Athletic Director, and Executive Associate Athletic Director) – An associate or assistant athletic director typically reports directly to the athletic director and is responsible for one or more administrative areas within the department. For example, an associate athletic director for external affairs could have direct oversight over marketing, development, and media relations within the athletics department. An associate director for internal affairs could have direct oversight over compliance, academics, and student support. Major universities typically have several assistant or associate athletic directors, while small colleges might not have any mid-level administrators. **Experience:** A college degree is required and a master's degree is preferred. Previous experience in college athletics is also necessary.

**Business Manager** – The business manager is responsible for managing all financial aspects of the athletic department. This includes preparing and monitoring of budgets, preparing and analyzing financial statements, payroll records, forecasting and monitoring of revenues, forecasting and monitoring of expenditures, oversight of equipment purchasing, and oversight of departmental travel. **Experience:** A college degree is required in accounting or business administration. Previous experience in accounting in higher education is preferred.

**Marketing/Promotions** – The marketing director is responsible for developing marketing strategies for increasing attendance, revenue, support, and visibility for the athletic department. This includes the coordination of advertising campaigns, corporate sponsorships, ticket sales campaigns, licensing of products, and promotional activities. **Experience:** A college degree in business or marketing is required and a master's degree in sports management is preferred. Previous experience in marketing or sales is necessary.

**Academic Affairs** – The director of academic affairs is responsible for the monitoring of academic progress of the student-athletes, academic advising and counseling of the student-athletes, coordinating the tutorial programs, monitoring academic eligibility, maintaining accurate and complete academic records, and career development. **Experience:** A college degree is required and a master's degree or doctoral degree is preferred. Previous experience in academic advising is also preferred.

**Compliance** – The compliance officer is responsible for the oversight of all aspects of conference and national rules (i.e. NCAA rules) for the athletics department. This includes the oversight of the initial and continuing eligibility of student-athletes, the monitoring of financial aid, the interpretation and application of conference and NCAA legislation, rules education, preparing eligibility waivers, and maintaining appropriate compliance monitoring procedures. **Experience:** A college degree is required and a master's degree is preferred. Previous experience in college athletics is also preferred.

**Sports Information** (Another title can include Director of Media Relations) – The sports information director is also known as the director of media relations. He/she is responsible for the development (writing and layout) of the sports media guides and game programs, the writing and sending of news releases, staging press conferences, maintaining team and individual statistics, photography, and maintenance of the department's website. The SID quite often assists the marketing office with layout and design of promotional pieces such as the schedule cards, posters, ticket brochures, and advertisements. **Experience:** A college degree is required and previous experience in sports information is necessary. It is also preferred that the person have experience in writing, layout design, and maintaining of sports statistics.

**Fund Raising/Development** – An athletics development officer is responsible for the fundraising activities within the athletics department. This includes the identification, cultivation, solicitation, and stewardship of all philanthropic gifts to the athletic department. This position is also responsible for the direction and oversight of the annual fund (booster club), any special fundraising events such as a golf tournament or an auction, and planned-giving. **Experience:** A college degree is required and a master's degree is preferred. Previous experience in fund raising or sales is also preferred.

**Ticket Manager** – The ticket manager is responsible for managing the sale and distribution of game tickets. This includes the printing of the tickets, selling of the tickets, maintaining accurate inventories, distribution of the tickets, and reconciliation of both the tickets and the money from the sale of tickets. **Experience:** A college degree is required. Previous experience working in a ticket office is also necessary.

**Equipment Manager** – The equipment manager is responsible for the purchasing, maintenance, inventory control, and record keeping of the equipment used by the sports teams. This is a real hands on position that will include the daily pickup of practice gear, cleaning the gear, and distributing it back to the teams for their next practice. The equipment manager needs to be extremely organized and have strict control over the access and security of the equipment. **Experience:** Previous experience working in an equipment room is preferred.

**Facilities Manager** – This is sometimes also referred to as the facilities and events manager, or the operations manager. This person is responsible for the scheduling of the athletics facilities, the maintenance of the facilities, and managing of the events within the facilities. They will also be responsible for the budgeting and fiscal management of the facilities, the rental of facilities, and managing of the rental contracts. This position typically supervises a relatively large staff of maintenance and event personnel. **Experience:** A college degree is required, typically in business administration. Previous experience in facilities management is also preferred.

**Athletic Trainer** – An athletic trainer is the sports medicine professional within the athletic department. They are responsible for managing the prevention, care, and rehabilitation of athletic injuries. They attend practices and games so they can provide medical coverage for the athletes. In many colleges, the athletic trainer will teach in the physical education department.

In addition, the athletic trainer is quite often the coordinator of medical insurance for the athletic department. **Experience:** A college degree is required in exercise science or athletic training. NATA certification, first aid certification, and CPR certification is required. A master's degree is preferred.

**Strength Coach** – A strength and conditioning coach is responsible for creating, implementing and administering a comprehensive strength and conditioning program for designated athletes and teams. He/she manages and supervises the athletic weight room, and develops strict policies and procedures for safe handling of the equipment. They also are responsible for the supervision and purchasing of weight-room equipment. **Experience:** A college degree is required in physical education or exercise science, and a master's degree is preferred.

## Positions in a College Recreation Department

**Recreation Director** – The recreation director is responsible for the operation and programming of the entire recreation department. This includes oversight of intramural activities, club sports, the aquatics program, outdoor recreation, wellness programs, and facilities management. **Experience:** A master's degree in recreation, leisure studies, physical education, or sports management is required. Previous managerial experience in recreation is necessary.

**Outdoor Recreation** – The coordinator of outdoor recreation manages the daily operation of the outdoor recreational programs. This includes coordinating, event planning, and execution of all of the outdoor activities. These activities include programs such as camping, hiking, kayaking, climbing, and wilderness training. The outdoor recreation coordinator is also responsible for purchasing and maintaining the equipment used in the outdoor program. **Experience:** A bachelor's degree and previous experience working in an outdoor recreation program is usually required.

**Intramural Sports** – The intramural director/coordinator is responsible for the development, coordination, marketing, and operation of the intramural sports program. He/she will plan the events, promote them to the students, and assure the successful operation of each sports activity. At large universities this position might have a staff of employees, whereas, at a small to medium sized college this position is quite often combined with another position such as a coach. **Experience:** A bachelor's degree is usually required.

**Club Sports** – This position is quite often an administrative assistant type position within the recreation department, or is combined with another position such as the intramural director. The coordinator of club sports provides coordination and communication with each of the club sports, their campus advisor, and with the associated students who usually sponsor the club activities. **Experience:** A bachelor's degree is preferred.

**Facilities Manager** – A facilities manager is responsible for the operation of the fitness facilities and is often a position within the recreation department. At a major university, this position has a staff that they manage, whereas, at the small to medium size college these duties are usually combined with the director of recreation. The facilities manager will oversee the construction, maintenance, scheduling, and rental of all indoor and outdoor recreation facilities. **Experience:** A bachelor's degree is required and a master's degree is preferred. Previous experience is also required.

**Aquatics Director** – The aquatics director oversees the planning, scheduling, operations, and supervision of the pool. This includes supervision of recreational swim, teaching swim lessons, and providing lifeguard training. At a large university, this is a full-time position. However, at a small to medium size college this position is usually combined with the swim coach position. **Experience:** A bachelor's degree is required. Certifications are also required in first aid, CPR, AED, and water safety instruction.

**Fitness Manager** – Many recreation departments offer fitness programs that can be both for credit or non-credit. They can include evening and/or weekend type programming. Fitness programming can include activities such as dance, walking, weight lifting, self-defense, and step aerobics. Quite often the manager of the fitness program also oversees the wellness program. **Experience:** A bachelor's degree is usually required in exercise physiology or physical education. Previous experience is also preferred.

**Wellness Director** – The wellness director is responsible for the coordinating and organizing of the health and wellness program. This includes producing seminars and programs in weight management, nutrition, fitness classes, and healthy lifestyle programs. The wellness director is often combined with the fitness manager. **Experience:** A master's degree is typically required in physical education, health, or nutrition. Previous experience is also preferred.

# CHAPTER 2

## Job Search Strategies in College Sports

Chapter One provided an overview of the types of sports-related jobs that are available in college coaching, athletic administration, recreation, and organizations that are affiliated with college sports. But how does a person get their start in the profession and how do they move up in their career? With both coaching and administration there is not one exact right way to proceed. However, there are certain strategies that a person can utilize that will help them in their career. The sections that follow will provide some insights for you to ponder so that you can investigate to see which career path is right for you. This chapter will provide suggestions for (a) breaking into the industry, (b) moving up in the industry, and (c) getting back into the profession.

Working in college sports can be extremely fulfilling. As with most professions, college sports will require a certain amount of sacrifice and perseverance in order to break into and advance within the industry. But the fact remains the same, coaching sports and administering sport programs at the college level can be some of the most fulfilling professions in the world. This book provides strategies and techniques that can assist a person as they begin to break into the sports profession and as they advance within the industry.

## Breaking into the Profession

Sometimes breaking into college sports is difficult for a person and sometimes it seems as if the person is at the right place at the right time. Either way, breaking into the business of college sports requires passion for sports, a strong work ethic, sacrifices, and maybe a little luck. How difficult it is to break into a particular position will depend largely upon the level of competition, the salary, and the type of position. As you can imagine, it is easier to become a volunteer assistant coach in an Olympic sport at a small college, than it is to become a full-time assistant coach at the Division I level in football or basketball.

Regardless of the type of job that you seek within sports, there is not one right way to break into the profession of coaching or sports management. If you know what your career goals are, you will want to develop a "road map" for your career by working through the *Career Planning Guide* in Chapter Five. If, however, you do not know what your career goals are, but you know that you want to work in the field of college sports, you then need to ask a lot of questions and work through the various assessments in Chapter Four. Through the use of assessments and tests, you will attempt to identify the area or the type of position within college sports that interests you. Once you have identified the type of position that interests you, you will plan your career using the planning guide in Chapter Five. If, however, you are still confused about the type of job that you want, the best thing to do is to get an entry-level position with either an athletic department or a recreation department and explore the various career options. As you gain experience in the profession, you will develop a better understanding of the type of job that interests you. At that point, you will want to update your planning guide to reflect your interests and goals.

So how exactly do you break into college athletics? There is no one exact way, but by meeting people and asking questions, furthering your academic and professional experiences, volunteering, interning, and networking, you will be heading in the right direction. The *Career Planning Guide* in Chapter Five and the networking section in Chapter Eight will help provide some guidance. Also, the section below provides some suggestions on strategies that you might want to consider.

## Strategies for Breaking into Coaching

As you begin to break into the college coaching ranks there are three broad areas that you will need to focus on: (a) learn all that you can about your sport, (b) begin to network within the industry, and (c) gain experience. Below are some strategies for breaking into the profession of college coaching. Review each of these suggestions and include whichever ones are appropriate for you as you develop your strategy for breaking into coaching at the college level.

### Learn All That You Can

Beginning your career in college coaching is an exciting time. You will need to prepare yourself to eventually become an expert in your sport. With this in mind, it is imperative that you study everything you can about your sport. Learn the proper skills and techniques. Learn the strategies and schemes. And learn everything you can about developing a sports program.

**Coaching Philosophy** – As you read and learn about your sport, you will need to develop a coaching philosophy. This philosophy will guide you as you move through your career. In developing your coaching philosophy, you will first want to adopt the right core values that will help you to be successful as a coach. Ask yourself some key questions such as, why do you want to coach? What are your strengths that you bring to the profession? What are your weaknesses?

Your core values could include such items as having a strong work ethic, having passion for the profession, helping student-athletes to grow and develop, having the desire to teach, continuing to learn, and operating with integrity. The next area of your philosophy is the sport itself. What skills and techniques will you emphasize? What types of offenses and defenses will you implement? What is your style of play? Your core values and strategies will help guide you as you continue to grow and move in your career.

**Clinics** – In order for you to gain knowledge about your future profession, it is important that you begin to surround yourself with other coaches by attending coaching clinics. Coaching clinics have expert coaches who speak about their sport and they discuss the techniques that are utilized in the sport. Be active at these clinics. Ask questions and introduce yourself to other coaches. This is a great opportunity for you to learn and grow.

**X & O** – X & Oing is strategizing and diagramming techniques, methods, and plays with other coaches. It is critical for young coaches to increase their knowledge of their sport, while getting to know other coaches. Ask other coaches to share their thoughts on a certain out-of-bounds play, on proper techniques for effective tackling, or on anything you are curious about. This will not only help to increase your knowledge of your sport, but it is also one of the best methods for networking.

**Read Books/Watch Videos** – It is critical that you learn the basic techniques of your sport and how to properly teach these techniques. There are many books, magazines, and videos on the market that discuss all aspects of coaching such as what are the basic fundamental techniques of your sport, how to teach these techniques, how to organize practices, how to motivate your student-athletes, and how to develop a cohesive team. These are just a few of the many topics that you need to learn as you move forward in this profession.

## Establishing A Coaching Network

Most people get jobs in coaching as a direct result of knowing people who know the head coach. It cannot be overemphasized how important it is to network and to get to know other coaches. However, keep in mind that networking is not about getting to know people just so they will help you to get a job. Networking is building friendships and relationships with others in your profession. These friendships should be a two-way street where you help each other with advice, strategy, and emotional support. Below are some ways to begin to network within your profession. Chapter Eight will discuss networking in much greater detail.

**Informational Interview** – Many people begin their networking by having an informational interview. An informational interview is where a person will interview an established and experienced coach in order to learn more about the industry. You will want to begin the process by contacting a coach and asking if you can meet with them to find out more about the coaching profession. Ask them questions about their job, their duties, about how to break into the profession, etc. Do not, however, ask them for a job during the first meeting. This could make them feel as if you were insincere in your desire to meet, and that you had ulterior motives. Follow-up this meeting with a thank you letter and let them know that you will keep them abreast of your progress. This is the key for building a relationship. Then follow through and periodically stay in touch with them by updating them on your progress.

**Summer Camps** – Working summer camps is a great way to network. Camps allow a person to show their colleagues how hard they work, how passionate they are about their sport, what their personality is like, and how competent they are within their sport. As much as anything else, working summer camps allows you to really get to know other coaches in much greater depth.

**Clinics** – This was listed above as a way to improve your knowledge of your sport, but clinics are also a great way to begin to network. At sports clinics, a person has the opportunity to interact with a lot of other coaches. You have the opportunity to build friendships with these coaches and stay in touch with them throughout your career. If you have the chance to have lunch or dinner with other coaches during a break, take advantage of this time. Again, this is a great opportunity to get to know others within the profession and to build friendships.

**Watching a Practice** – Ask a coach if you can watch one of their practices. This will allow you to visit with the coaching staff in a comfortable and non-threatening setting. You can really learn a lot from watching other coaches run a practice, but more so, you can also really get to know the coaching staff.

## Gaining Experience in Coaching

Keep in mind that having a successful career in any profession is a journey and not a race. Building a career takes time if done correctly. Be patient and work your way up. Prove yourself as a passionate and professional coach. Below are some ways people are able to gain experience within the coaching profession.

**Graduate Assistant** – Going back to graduate school and coaching while in school is a popular way to break into the profession. Many coaches have gotten their start by pursuing their master's degree and serving as a graduate assistant coach. Having a master's degree is almost a necessity to becoming a college coach. Sometimes graduate assistantships are paid a stipend and sometimes they are not. Search the classifieds such as the *NCAA* website and the *Chronicle of Higher Education* for potential leads. Ask coaches if they know of any assistantships that will be opening soon.

**Volunteer Assistant** – One of the best ways to break into the coaching profession is to become a volunteer assistant. If you do become a volunteer, make sure that you work hard to prove that you are serious about becoming a college coach.

**Small College Assistant** – Many smaller colleges need assistant coaches. An assistant's position at a small college quite often starts out as a volunteer coach.

**Student Assistant** – If you are an undergraduate student and not participating on the team in the sport that you want to coach someday, approach the head coach to see if you can help them as an assistant, as a manager, or in some capacity. Let them know that you want to be a coach and that you would appreciate his/her guidance and advice. If you are given the opportunity, take advantage of it and work hard. Do every project in a first-rate manner. Always be punctual, and ask a lot of questions. This is a great opportunity.

**High School Coach** – Working as a high school coach, whether as a head coach or assistant coach, is a great way to gain experience. If this is the route that you take, your next step is to network into a full-time college assistant position or a graduate assistant coaching position. The keys are to gain experience, to network, and to position yourself for a college coaching position.

**Junior High Coach** – If you cannot break into the profession in any of the above scenarios, try to break in by working at the junior high level. The main key is for you to gain experience. A year at the junior high level can lead to a position at the high school level, or as a volunteer at a college.

## Case Study #1
### Breaking into College Coaching

Randy Brown grew up in north central Iowa in the community of Fort Dodge. From the time he can remember, he was passionate about the game of basketball. His lifelong dream was to coach basketball at the college level. After a successful high school basketball career, Randy went on to play two years of college basketball at Iowa Central Community College.

Upon graduating from the community college, he set his sights on finishing his bachelor's degree and breaking into the profession of coaching. His passion for the game of basketball took him to the University of Iowa where he would finish up his degree and would look to get his start in coaching.

In his two years in Iowa City, Randy became a volunteer assistant coach at Regina High School, and he attended almost every basketball practice the University of Iowa Hawkeye's had. He got to know the Hawkeye's head coach, Lute Olson, and got to know the assistant coaches.

Every day at the Hawkeye's practice, Randy would write down everything he could learn. He diagramed the drills, the plays, and the practice plans. He asked questions and wrote down the answers. He was like a sponge in that he soaked up every experience he could. It paid off, after graduating with a degree in physical education Randy became an assistant coach at Pleasant Valley High School, just north of the Quad Cities.

Randy spent three years in that position, while continuing to be aggressive and active in networking and learning all he could about the game. His hard work and networking was beginning to pay dividends when Lute Olson hired Randy to become a graduate assistant at Arizona. This move would eventually catapult his career as he became an assistant at the University of North Dakota, then at Drake, then at Marquette, until he became a Division I head coach at Stetson University.

Today, Randy is helping others to break into the industry by providing a mentoring service for young coaches. But it was his passion, hard work, and sacrifice that helped him to break into the industry, and paved the way for a successful career.

# Strategies for Breaking into Sports Administration

There are a lot of similarities in how a person could break into either college coaching or sports administration. Many of the techniques and suggestions are the same because they are the best methods for breaking into any profession. Below are some of the strategies for breaking into the profession of administration within college sports. Review each of these suggestions and include whichever ones are appropriate for you as you develop your strategies for breaking into sports administration.

**Informational Interviews** – A good way to gain more information about the industry is to schedule an informational interview. An informational interview is where a person who is looking to break into an industry will meet with someone who is experienced within the industry in an attempt to gain knowledge about the profession. To schedule an informational interview, you should call, or send an e-mail, to the person who you want to interview and ask them if they would be available sometime for an informational interview. Explain that you are trying to break into the industry and that you want to learn as much as you can about the profession. Make sure that you are prepared with the questions that you want to ask. Since you are the one who scheduled the meeting, you will be the person conducting the interview. Be considerate of their time and do not exceed an hour (maybe even 20-30 minutes). You will want to follow-up this meeting by sending a personal letter, a note, or an e-mail so that you can properly thank them for their time.

**Master's Degree** – Consider going back to graduate school so you can pursue your master's degree in sports management. While in graduate school, you should volunteer and begin to gain experience within the industry. This is a great way to gain experience and break into the profession. You will want to go to a program that is well respected and where you can meet other future leaders. This is also a very good networking opportunity, plus a master's degree is becoming a necessity for moving up in the profession.

**Volunteer** – Another great way to break into college sports is to volunteer in an athletic department. There are always opportunities in game management, security, ticket sales, and marketing. This would be a great question to ask in an informational interview – Are there any opportunities to volunteer in the department in order to gain experience? Who should I contact? If you do volunteer, make sure you do a great job; your reputation is at stake and you will want a letter of recommendation or a reference someday.

**Entry-level Job** – Get an entry-level job such as selling tickets, taking tickets, or keeping statistics during the team's contests. Ask the ticket manager, the marketing director, or the sports information director if they ever hire for entry-level positions, or if they hire part-time positions during the home contests. Again, if you are hired, do a great job. Make yourself invaluable. You just might find yourself being hired in a full-time position in that particular athletic department.

**Internship** – Seek out an internship. These are usually in conjunction with your studies during your undergraduate degree program or your master's degree program. Some internships pay a stipend, but many do not – they just provide the experience.

**Network into a job** – As you have probably discovered, networking is the key to getting a job. Utilize the above opportunities and techniques to get to know people and then stay in touch with them and build friendships.

## Moving Up in The Profession

Getting a start in the profession of college sports is probably the hardest stage in your career. Now that you have started your career, what is the best strategy for advancement within the profession? To advance in any career you need to position yourself as a desirable commodity. In the world of college athletics, you need to have the proper educational training, develop the skills necessary for success in the profession, and gain the necessary experience for advancement. The *Career Planning Guide* in Chapter Five will help provide you with a step-by-step worksheet to plan out your career.

As you move forward in your career, reflect back to how Randy Brown approached his career in college basketball. He attended every practice the Hawkeyes had and he wrote down everything he could learn about the profession. As a graduate assistant, he joined the coaches' association (the NABC), he attended the national conventions, and he quickly became known for his work ethic and professionalism. You too need to take this attitude and work ethic to your career. Get involved in your national association. Write articles on topics within your profession and get them published in your trade journals and publications. Get to know everything there is about your profession. Get to know the leaders within the profession. Be a commodity within your profession, and be in a position for that next job when it becomes available. If you approach your career with excellence, you will definitely advance in your career.

## Strategies for Moving Up in Coaching

There are many strategies that can assist you in moving up in the coaching profession. Whichever strategy or strategies you choose, you will want to establish a plan as to how you will accomplish your goals for moving up. For example, if you want to improve your network within the profession, how do you plan to accomplish this? Will you begin to target a certain group of people and then meet with them so you can get to know them? It is best to write down your plans and include action steps and time frames for your plans. Below are eight strategies for moving up in the profession.

**Work Hard** – There is no substitute for a strong work ethic. Having a strong work ethic is a necessity if you are going to advance in the industry. There are many people who are hard workers in the coaching industry and you will need to be a hard worker just to keep up.

**Network** – As you move forward within your coaching career, you will want to continue to network with other coaches. As you advance in your career, sometimes a person's effort in networking begins to fade. Make sure to keep your network active. Make a concerted effort to stay current with other coaches by sending them a periodic e-mail (or call them) to see how they are doing or to congratulate them on the birth of a child (or a major life event). Be social with other coaches at clinics, camps and conventions.

**Brand Yourself** – As you gain experience as a coach you will begin to become "branded" or known for your reputation. Do people see you as a good recruiter, a knowledgeable coach, a hard worker, a professional, or maybe as just getting by. Focus on the brand that you want and work hard to accomplish it.

**Become A Great Recruiter** – Recruiting is the life-blood of a college sports program. Work on becoming the very best recruiter you can be. You might want to take an executive sales course or a speaking course from a professional who specializes in these areas. For example, Patricia Fripp at Fripp and Associates provides this type of service. Toastmasters is another possible association that can provide services to improve your interpersonal communication skills. There are many organizations that provide sales training.

**Win More Games** – Schedule appropriately, recruit a higher-level player, study and focus on execution for both practices and games. This is easier said than done, but by taking a course on executive sales you can improve your presentation skills and become a better recruiter. You can also create a schedule that is appropriate for the quality of team you expect to have. For example, if you have a young team, schedule an easier non-conference schedule. Conversely, if you have a more experienced squad, create a little tougher schedule. I would never recommend, however, that you create such a tough schedule that you do not have a chance to win at least half of your non-conference games.

**Seek Advice** – Seek advice from the very best in the profession. Introduce yourself to them and ask if you could visit with them and "pick their brain". Most coaches are open to sharing their information. If the coach does not want to meet, do not take it personally and move on to the next coach. However, if you really want to visit with this particular coach, be persistent (but not obnoxious) in trying to visit with them.

**Execute** – Learn to execute the basics of your sport. How many times does an untimely turnover or penalty cost your team at the most crucial stage of the game? Study the basics of how to execute the skills of the game.

**Successful Job Search** – Learn how to conduct a successful job search. There is definitely a technique to learn and these techniques will help you as you attempt to move up in the profession.

## Strategies for Moving Up in Sports Administration

There are many strategies that a person can use to accelerate their moving up in the profession of administration within college sports. Below are seven of these strategies. Review each of these strategies and choose which ones could fit into your plan for advancing your career.

**Networking** – By now you should be developing a strong network. Many people, however, get too busy to take the time to network effectively. Do not fall into this trap. Continue to send out letters, make telephone calls, and build relationships. Also, make sure that you attend the professional conferences and conventions. The NACDA convention is the main convention for sports administrators.

**Quality Work** – If you do quality work it will be noticed. It will also be noticed if you do not do a quality job. The industry is a very small fraternity and you are building your reputation (and brand) on how hard you work and on the quality of your work.

**Work Hard** – There is no substitute for a strong work ethic. Having a strong work ethic is a necessity if you are going to advance in the industry. There are many people who are hard workers within the sports industry, and you will need to work hard just to keep up.

**Brand Yourself** – As you get further into your career, you will begin to become "branded" or known for your reputation. Do people see you as a great marketer, a good fundraiser, a hard worker, a professional, or maybe as just getting by. Focus on the brand that you want and work hard to accomplish the reputation associated with this brand.

**Becoming an Expert** – As a part of branding yourself, you will want to become known as an expert within your profession. You will want to specialize in a segment of the industry and be active in your professional association. As an expert, you will want to write articles and become a speaker at your professional conferences.

**Help Others to Advance** – Most likely someone has helped you to get into the industry and to advance in your career. You in turn should be open to helping others to advance as well. Not only is this the right thing to do, it can only come back to help you someday.

**Be Patient** – Too often people try to advance too quickly in the industry. Do quality work, work hard, and your opportunities will come. When the timing is right to move on, you will know. Get to know the strategies in this book so when it is time to move on, you will be ready.

## Getting Back into the Profession

Getting back into the profession after you have stepped away for a while, either by your own choice or not, can be very difficult. Many coaches and administrators find themselves having been displaced and wanting to get back into the business.

If your contract was not renewed, there are probably some hurt feelings. This is a natural emotion. However, the first step to getting back on your feet and back into the profession is to let go of any hurt feelings. This is a must before you can begin to move forward. Forgiving the people who led to your resignation is the first step to positioning yourself for your next job. Research has shown that people who are still harboring hurt feelings and anger are placing their energies in the wrong place. Searching for a job is, in itself, a full-time job, and you must have your full attention in the process. Plus, put yourself in the position of the hiring manager. Would you want to hire someone who is bitter and unfocused?

However, be realistic in where you can get back in and at what level. Typically, a person will need to take a position that is a step down in order to stay in the profession. For example, a head coach who has been displaced might want to take an assistant's position at the same level, or another head coaching position at a lower level. The coach will then need to refocus his or her career and readjust their goals.

The chapters ahead will provide you with an organized method for conducting an effective job search. This includes building a great resume, cover letter, knowledge on how to answer interview questions, and how to follow-up after the interview with a strategy that gives you the best possible chance of being hired. Not every concept in this book will help everyone, however if only one or two of these concepts can help out, this book has been worthwhile.

## Strategies for Getting Back into the Profession

Do not compromise your values just to get back into the profession. By continuing to network, to improve your knowledge of your specialization, and to learn how to search for a job, you will most likely get back into the profession. But never compromise your values and integrity. What you stand for (e.g. your reputation, your image, your brand) is critical for getting hired again. Below are some ideas and strategies to assist you as you work to get back into the sports industry.

**Network** – At this stage of your career, networking is going to be a key to getting back into the profession. Continue to keep your networking ties active. Do not be hesitant in letting your friends know what type of job you desire. Do not assume that they know. They will be very important in helping you to get interviews and influencing those who are making the hire.

**Improve Your Deficiencies** – It is important that you understand why your previous job was terminated (if it was). It might have just been a bad fit, or it could have been a political struggle. Whatever the reason, learn from the situation and work to strengthen your weaknesses. Everyone has strengths and weaknesses. What are your weaknesses? Work to improve in those areas. Take an executive sales course. Attend more coaching clinics. Get better so a prospective employer will want to hire you. Above all, **stay positive!** Being displaced is frustrating and it is easy to be negative. However, if you were the hiring manager, do you want to hire a negative person who is feeling sorry for themselves, or do you want to hire that upbeat, positive, professional?

**Learn Strategies to Get a Job** – It is important that you learn, or brush up on, job search strategies. You will want to learn the latest interviewing skills and techniques. Even if you think you know these skills, it will not hurt you to brush up on them. By learning job search strategies, you will speed up the time it takes to get back into the profession. This book should help you learn the techniques that are necessary to conduct a successful job search.

**Position Yourself** – It is important to put yourself in a position to get back into the profession or into the right job within the profession. This means that the job you are searching for should put you in a position where your next job (or two jobs from now) is the job you truly want. For example, if you are attempting to return as an athletic director at the Division I level, holding out for a Division I athletic director's job might be unrealistic at this time. However, look at a Division II athletic director's position or at a Division I associate athletic director's position. These could "position" you to get that Division I athletic director's job in the future. The *Career Planning Guide* in Chapter Five will be critical for helping you to plan out what type of position you should be searching for now, in an attempt to position yourself for your next job.

**Stay Active** – It is also important that you stay active in the profession while you are attempting to get back in. The last thing you need is a gap in your resume. Quite often a gap can be hard to explain. However, if you become a consultant within the industry, or assist a consultant, it will be easier to explain the change. This does not mean that the consulting job will pay the bills; it might just help with the resume. In fact, you might not make a dime as a consultant. Maybe you will want to get a paying job (doing whatever) during the day and moonlight as a consultant by night. You might decide to write articles for publication as your project, or you might want to ask a friend in the industry if you could analyze their department for free, just so you have a project you can list on your resume. Whatever you decide to do, find a way to stay active in the profession and to fill the gap in your resume.

## Case Study #2
### Getting Back into the Profession

Intercollegiate Athletics can be very political at times. This can be seen with the career of Dick Dull. Dick was on the fast track as the Athletic Director at the University of Maryland at a relatively young age. He became the Terrapin's Athletic Director while in his mid-30's. During his fifth year at the helm, one of the star men's basketball players died on campus in a dorm room. The repercussions were the resignation of a quality athletic director and that of the head men's basketball coach. Of course, these two people were not involved in any way with the player's death, but as the leaders of the program they were caught in a "political realignment."

Now Dick was in his early 40's and still had a good 20-30 years of service he could provide to an institution and their student-athletes. Dick had a reputation of being a great person and a quality administrator. However, he elected to stay out of the industry for nearly 10 years. When he decided to return to college athletics, the question came up – at what level does a former athletic director of an ACC school get back in? A person undoubtedly does not start back as an ACC athletic director again. Dick was a great fit at the Division I level but it would take a few more years of proper positioning of himself and quality work for him to land at the Division I level again.

In 1995 Dick returned to athletics as the Director of Athletics at the University of Nebraska at Kearney. He did an outstanding job during his three years there and he was able to move up in the industry. In essence, he positioned himself for his next position. Dick was hired as the Athletic Director at Moravian College in 1998 because of his reputation as a quality administrator and his impeccable integrity. It took just a year and a half at Moravian before a Division I school came knocking on his door. He was hired as the Athletic Director at California State University at Northridge in May of 1999.

Dick finished his career as the Athletic Director at Belmont Abbey, a school that is closer to his family on the east coast. He recently retired after an outstanding career and positively impacting the lives of many people. His story is not unusual for an athletic director or coach. The smart thing that Dick did in getting back into the industry was he took a job at a lower division, and positioned himself for his next move. It only took him four-plus years to return to the Division I level.

*CHAPTER 3*

---

# The Job Search Process

In the previous chapters you were introduced to the types of jobs that exist in college sports. These include positions in college athletics, recreational sports, and organizations that support the various coaching and administration positions. You were also introduced to the three primary reasons why a person searches for a job – to break into the industry, to move up in the profession, or to get back into the profession. From there, various strategies where presented that could assist you with getting hired and advancing within the profession.

Every person's situation and background is a little bit different, but the basic elements of the job search process are the same for everyone. For most people, the job search process includes submitting a cover letter and a resume for a job that is being advertised and then waiting to hear back from the employer. If the employer calls and wants to set-up an interview, most people will then prepare and be ready to sell themselves. However, these are not the best methods for securing a job. Through extensive research, the proper job search process has been identified and is outlined in the following chapters. This process will help lead you to an organized and strategic search and ultimately to securing the job you want.

## The Process

*The Sports-Related Job Search Model* was introduced in the first edition of *Getting Hired in College Sports*. The model is the culmination of extensive research and is designed to help people in their job searches by creating a job search process that is organized, systematic, and strategic. The Sports-Related Job Search Model is shown in Figure 1 on the next page.

As the model shows, there are two phases to a job search – the Discovery Phase and the Search Phase. In the Discovery Phase the goal is to understand your strengths and skills, and discover the job or career that is right for you. This might be accomplished during the Self-Assessment Stage or it might be necessary to also complete the Testing Stage. Once the Discovery Phase is completed, you now have a focus for the type of career you are looking for, and you will enter the Search Phase.

The Search Phase is a continual loop of preparing for your job search, making contact with potential employers, interviewing for jobs, and following up after the interview. This process will continue until the right job is accepted. Each of these four stages will be thoroughly discussed in the chapters that follow.

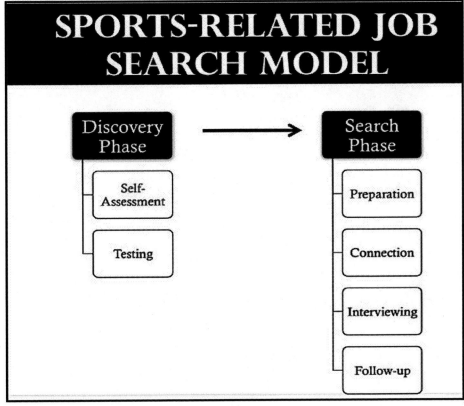

Figure 1. The Sports-Related Job Search Model

# Discovery Phase

As mentioned in the previous section, the Discovery Phase is comprised of both self-assessments and taking tests. In the discovery process, you will assess your skills, plan your career, and pinpoint the organizations where you would like to work. Some of these steps may seem elementary to you, but they will help you to reflect upon who you are and what you can provide an employer.

## Self-Assessment Stage

The initial part of the Discovery Phase of the job search process is the Self-Assessment Stage. The goal of the self-assessments is for you to get to know yourself and to provide yourself with a vision for your career. The results of these assessments will help to provide you with the answers to who you are and where you are going. You will evaluate your strengths, weaknesses, experiences, and goals, and then identify the organizations (target market) where you want to work. With a target market, you will identify the type of job you are searching for and the types of organizations where you would like to work. In the Self-Assessment Stage the following items will be discovered:

- Your occupational values – what you like and dislike in a job
- Your top five skills and abilities
- Your top personal traits
- A roadmap to achieving your dream job
- Figuring out which organizations to contact

## Testing Stage

The Testing Stage is discussed in Chapter Four along with the assessments that you will take. Two categories of tests are discussed – personality tests and career (aptitude) tests. Typically, a licensed counselor or a psychologist must administer most personality tests. However, a career counselor can assist you with most aptitude tests. Career tests tend to measure a person's aptitude for a skill or particular interest, whereas a personality test measures a person's behavior, thoughts, and feelings. Both personality tests and aptitude tests can be taken either on-line through various websites, or in person with the appropriate professional.

# Search Phase

The Search Phase is a continuous loop of preparation, making contact, interviewing, and following-up. Within this process a person can either be in a sampling mode or a full-blown campaign. A sampling mode is when a person periodically sends out a resume or is active in maintaining networking contacts. A full-blown campaign is when a person is actively searching for a job. In a campaign, a person will use various methods to locate jobs, and to make contacts. Also during a campaign, the person searching for a position will have several potential opportunities or applications going on at the same time.

## Preparation Stage

The Preparation Stage helps you to become organized in your search. It will help you to identify the organizations within your target market and then to develop the corresponding materials to market yourself. Also during the Preparation Stage, you will develop strategies for conducting a successful search. The following topics will be discussed in chapters five, six, and seven:

- Establish a target market contact list
- Build your resume
- Create a personal sales pitch
- Write a professional cover letter
- Establish a strategic list of references
- Develop strategies and answers to the most popular interview questions
- Research the organizations within your target market
- Develop an interview preparation form

## Connection Stage

The second section of the Search Phase is entitled the Connection Stage. In the connection stage, you will develop the promotional campaign for your job search: who to contact, how to contact, and when to contact them. There are various methods to use to make contact with potential employers, but two methods have been shown to be the most successful – networking and direct contact.

Other methods will be discussed as well. The final part of this stage is in controlling your search. The Connection Stage will be discussed in greater detail in Chapter Eight and will include the following topics:

- Developing a job search campaign
- Networking
- How to promote yourself
- Which promotional techniques to use
- Creating your brand
- Creating a strategic marketing plan for yourself
- How to control your job search

## Interviewing Stage

The third section in the Search Phase is the Interviewing Stage where you will prepare for your interviews. Preparing for the interview is extremely important. This book will help you to prepare by providing interview tips, sample interview questions, and will help to prepare you for what to expect during your interview. The Interviewing Stage will provide you with the basics for interviewing, strategies and techniques for having a successful interview, and how to interview like a consultant. The following topics will be discussed in greater detail:

- The proper approach to interviewing
- Interviewing basics
- Group interviews
- Institutional information
- Asking questions in the interview
- Mistakes people make
- Successfully closing the interview

## Strategic Follow-up Stage

The final section of the Search Phase is the Strategic Follow-up Stage. Properly following up after an interview is the key to this process. It is what separates you from your competition and ultimately gets you the job. A strategy needs to be developed that will help you to influence the people who interviewed you.

In Chapter 10, follow-up strategies will be discussed in greater detail. The Strategic Follow-up Stage includes:

- Follow-up after the interview

- Addressing issues and concerns

- Creating a follow-up mini-campaign

- Letter writing

- Salary negotiation strategy

- Creating an organized method for keeping track of each search and the status of the search

# Where Should I Begin

Each of the stages within the job search process is important. However, depending upon your situation, you should identify which stage of the process is the proper place for you to begin. For example, if you already know what type of position or job you want, you might be able to skip the Self-Assessment Stage. However, it is recommended that you still conduct the self-assessments. This will help you to know what skills and traits you possess, so that you can use this information in your sales pitch. Answer the following questions to determine where you should begin.

# Which Stage Are You In?

By determining which of the four questions is closest to your situation, you can determine which stage is the best place for you to begin. It is highly recommended that you do not skip any stages because the better you know yourself, and the better you know the strategies, the more likely you are to land the job of your dreams.

**Questions**

1. I feel as if I am lost. I am not sure what type of job or career I want.

2. I think I know what type of job I want, but is there a type of job that I am better suited for?

3. I know what type of position is right for me, but I cannot get an interview.

4. I am getting interviews, but I cannot land the job.

**Where Should You Begin?**

If you answered #1 or #2, you need to initially focus on the testing and assessments. Once you have completed these stages, and have a better understanding of your career path, the planning in the search stage will begin. If you answered #3, it can only help you to read the sections on testing and assessments, but your greatest focus needs to be on preparing for your search. Finally, if you answered #4, you need to review the information regarding interviewing skills and your follow-up strategies. You also need to look to expand into different target markets.

Form 1.1

# Action Steps

This chapter provides an overview of the job search process. Within this process there are 10 sections that will help you to become organized in your job search. These 10 sections are combined to create a **Personal Job Search Binder**.

**Action Step** – Over the course of this book you will be asked to complete assignments and prepare promotional materials. At this point you will need to go to the office supplies store and purchase a two-inch 3-ring binder, 10 dividers, and labels for the dividers. Insert the dividers into the binder (your workbook binder) and label each of the dividers with the following titles:

Section 1: *Assessments*

Section 2: *Career Planning Guide*

Section 3: *Target Market*

Section 4: *Promotional Materials*

Section 5: *Sales Pitch*

Section 6: *Interview Preparation Form*

Section 7: *Interview Questions*

Section 8: *Promotional Campaign*

Section 9: *Interviewing Basics*

Section 10: *Strategic Follow-up*

For those people who lead busy lives and do not have the time to put together the binder and system themselves, or to save the time and hassle, you can purchase a Personal Job Search Binder, along with all of the forms included at Sports Leadership Publishing Company.

**Action Step** – Complete the form *"Which Stage Are You In"* and place it in Section One of your Workbook Binder (Form 1.1)

# CHAPTER 4

## Assessing Your Skills and Abilities

I n the previous chapter you were introduced to the job search process and to the two distinct phases of the process – the Discovery Phase and the Search Phase. The objective of the Discovery Phase is to help you determine what types of skills and abilities you possess, and help you to identify what types of jobs interest you. The Discovery Phase does this through the use of self-assessments and the use of various tests. This chapter focuses on the Discovery Phase and is designed to help you to understand what your strengths are, what skills and abilities you possess, and what type of job best fits these traits.

If you have a background or interest in college sports, you know that working in intercollegiate athletics can be a very exciting and rewarding career. However, it does not matter if you have played on a college sports team or not, the real key is that you have an interest and passion for college sports. To point you in the right direction, this chapter focuses more specifically on helping you figure out what type of career you want, and what strengths and abilities you possess. The first part of the chapter has you analyze your strengths, weaknesses, skills, talents, likes, and dislikes through the use of various self-assessment tools.

This is followed up with how and where to seek more extensive assistance through personality tests and/or career tests. The last part of the chapter summarizes all of your skills, abilities, and traits. These will be used later in the process when you are constructing your resume, cover letter, and your personal sales pitch.

# Self-Assessments

During the Self-Assessment Stage, you will assess your strengths, skills, and traits through the use of four assessment tools. Some of these assessment exercises may seem elementary to you, but these tools will help you to reflect upon who you are, and this in turn will help you to create a focus for your career.

In the Self-Assessment Stage, you will be asked to complete four assessments – The Sports-Related Occupational Values Assessment, the Skills and Traits Assessment, the List of Skills, and the Motivated Strengths and Enjoyable Activities Exercise. Upon completion of these, you will have a better understanding of who you are and where you are going.

## Sports-Related Occupational Values Assessment

The Sports-Related Occupational Values Assessment is an exercise to help you identify what values you like or dislike in a job. By identifying your likes and dislikes, you are much more likely to identify a job or career that matches your strengths and allows you to find a job that you truly enjoy.

Based after the Work-Related Values Assessment from the United States Department of Labor and the University of Minnesota[11], the Sports-Related Occupational Values Assessment helps you to identify the tasks that you like to do in a job. These tasks give you pleasure, enjoyment, and meaning. Most jobs involve a combination of likes and dislikes. By identifying the tasks that you like and dislike in a job, you should be able to identify a career that involves the tasks you will enjoy most. After you have identified your likes and dislikes, continue on by comparing these occupational values to the tasks associated with the various sports-related jobs that are listed later in the chapter. These job categories range from compliance to coaching and marketing to recreation. Upon completion of this assessment, turn to the *Assessment Summary Sheet* in the back of this chapter and list the four values that you like most, the four values that you dislike, and the types of jobs that interest you.

## Sports-Related Occupational Values Assessment

**Instructions:** Occupational values are those things that you like to do in a job. They give you pleasure, enjoyment, and meaning. Most jobs involve a combination of likes and dislikes. By identifying both what you like and dislike about a particular job, you should be able to better identify a career that involves the tasks that you enjoy the most. Review the tasks below. Place a check mark next to the four tasks or responsibilities that you like the most, and check marks next to the four values that you dislike the most. List your top four likes and dislikes at the bottom of this assessment.

Likes  Dislikes      Values

_____    _____**Public Speaking** – I enjoy making presentations to groups of people and to the media.

_____    _____**Work with Numbers** – I am a numbers person and I like working with numbers, fractions, and percentages.

_____    _____**Sales** – I enjoy selling products and recruiting people to participate in worthy causes.

_____    _____**Authority** – I prefer to be the boss.

_____    _____**High Salary** – I would like to work in a job where I can make a lot of money.

_____ _____**Teaching** – I enjoy teaching, coaching, and giving instructions.

_____ _____**Details** – I am a detail oriented person.

_____ _____**Public Interaction** – I prefer to have a job that has contact with the community.

_____ _____**Helping Others** – I enjoy working in a job where I can help others.

_____ _____**Security** – I prefer a job that is stable and relatively free from turnover.

_____ _____**Work with Young People** – I would like to work in a position where I can teach or interact with students.

_____ _____**Leadership** – I would like to work in a job where I can direct, manage, and supervise the activities of others.

_____ _____**Facilities Management** – I would like to work in a job where I coordinate schedules, manage facilities, and maintain safe and clean environments.

_____ _____**Writing** – I enjoy writing papers, articles, and human interest stories.

_____ _____**Accounting** – I enjoy working with budgets, financial statements, payroll, and financial planning.

_____ _____**Creativity** – I enjoy working in a job that allows me to use my imagination to find new ways of doing things.

_____ _____**Reports** – I enjoy work where I coordinate and complete projects and reports.

_____ _____**Legal Documents** – I am good at reading and understanding legal documents and legal wording.

_____ _____**Events Management** – I enjoy planning and staging events and activities.

_____ _____**Work Week** – I would like a job where I work 40 hours per week with very little overtime.

____    ____**Medical Support** – I enjoy working in the medical care industry providing care, prevention, and rehabilitation of injuries for student-athletes.

____    ____**Decisions** – I can make difficult decisions.

____    ____**Marketing** – I enjoy developing marketing strategies, and creating ways to promote our product.

____    ____**Recreation** – I enjoy organizing and staging sporting activities for students.

____    ____**Business Management**– I enjoy analyzing the effectiveness of an enterprise, its expenditures, its revenues, its profitability, and its use of resources.

____    ____**Equipment** – I am an organized person and I would enjoy ordering, organizing, maintaining, and keeping inventories of equipment.

## Tabulate Your Occupational Values

Select the four occupational values from the list above that you like doing the most. List these values in the "Likes" column. Next, select the four values that you dislike the most. List these values in the "Dislikes" column. If there are some values that are important to you that are not listed above, add them to the appropriate list. Finally, list your likes and dislikes in the *Assessment Summary Sheet* at the end of the chapter.

| Likes | Dislikes |
|-------|----------|
| 1. _____ | 1. _____ |
| 2. _____ | 2. _____ |
| 3. _____ | 3. _____ |
| 4. _____ | 4. _____ |

Form 1.2

As you begin to look at your likes and dislikes, a pattern may begin to surface. If your likes show that you are a detail oriented person who likes to work with numbers, accounting and reports, you probably would enjoy a position in business management. If, however, these types of duties are a turn-off, you would want to focus your attention in areas other than the business department. This is the process for how you will want to analyze your strengths and weaknesses.

The following list should help to provide you with some assistance in attempting to combine your likable values with the types of jobs that are available in the world of college sports. Compare the occupational values that you like with the sports-related jobs listed below. This comparison should assist in helping you to define the type of job that you would enjoy within college sports. Keep in mind that this is only one assessment. You will want to complete all four of the assessments so you can obtain a clear picture of the types of jobs that match your skills, abilities, and interests.

## Sports-Related Jobs

**Academic Advisor** – Details, teaching, helping others, work week.

**Athletic Training** – Teaching, details, helping others, security, work with young people, facilities management, and medical support.

**Associate/Assistant Athletic Director** – These positions will reflect the area of specialization (e.g. marketing, fund raising, operations, etc.).

**Athletic Director** – Public speaking, sales, authority, high salary, public interaction, leadership, facilities management, reports, legal documents, events management, marketing, decisions, business management.

**Business Manager** – Works with numbers, legal documents, authority, details, accounting, reports, business management.

**Coaching (Head Coach)** – Public speaking, sales (recruiting), authority, teaching, details, public interaction, helping others, work with young people, leadership, decisions, equipment.

**Coaching (Assistant Coach)** – Sales (recruiting), teaching, details, public interaction, helping others, work with young people.

**Compliance** – Details, security, reports, legal documents, work week.

**Development (Fund Raising)** – Public speaking, sales, details, public interaction.

**Equipment Management** – Details, security, events management, equipment.

**Facilities Management** – Authority, Details, security, leadership, facilities management, business management, events management, decisions, equipment.

**Marketing** – Public speaking, sales, public interaction, creativity, marketing, events management.

**Operations** – Details, business management, decisions, authority, facilities management, reports, legal documents.

**Promotions** – Sales, public interaction, creativity, marketing, events management.

**Recreation** – Security, work with young people, leadership, facilities management, events management, marketing, recreation, equipment.

**Sports Information (Media Relations)** – Public speaking, details, public interaction, work with young people, writing, creativity, events management, marketing.

**Strength and Conditioning** – Teaching, work with young people, medical support, and equipment.

**Student Support** – Teaching, details, helping others, security, work with young people, work week.

**Ticketing** – Work with numbers, sales, details, public interaction, security, reports.

Upon completion of this first assessment, you will want to list your findings (your four likes and dislikes) in the *Assessment Summary Sheet* at the end of this chapter. Then you will list the top three types of jobs that interest you. Remember that these are just your initial thoughts and you will not be locked into any particular type of job. For example, you might be interested in becoming an athletic director or a director of a recreation department, but you will not start at the top. Therefore, what other areas within college sports interests you? Maybe you are a good writer and like working with people. Your intermediary steps might be in the areas of media relations (also known as sports information), marketing, fund raising, or coaching. List these interests (likes, dislikes, and jobs) in the summary sheet at the end of the chapter. These interests will be used in the next chapter as you begin to develop your step-by-step career plan.

## Skills and Traits Assessment

The second assessment tool is the *Skills and Traits Assessment*. Carole Martin in her article, *Assessing Your Skills: What Makes You Different from All the Others?,* identified three types of skills for assessing your strengths – knowledge-based skills, transferable skills, and personal traits.[12] Knowledge-based skills are those you gain through experience and training. Transferable skills are those that can be transferred from one job to another, and personal traits are traits that make you unique. The Skills and Traits Assessment tool is based on these three skills. To see a sample list of skills, the third assessment, *List of Skills*, can provide you with details of some of life's basic skills.

The *Skills and Traits Assessment* provides you with a sampling of some of the traits and skills that a person might possess. The actual skills you possess might be, and probably are, different than those listed in the example. List as many skills or traits that you think you might possess. Upon completion of this exercise, list your top five skills and traits in the *Assessment Summary Sheet* in the back of this chapter. These will be used as you create your Personal Sales Pitch and your cover letter.

# Skills and Traits Assessment

**Directions:** List each of your skills and traits into one of the three categories below. Seek the opinion of someone close to you so that you make sure that you are not forgetting an important skill or trait. Knowledge-based skills are those that you have acquired through education and experience. Transferable skills are those that can be transferred from one industry to another. Personal traits are those that make you unique.

The following skills are an example of a person's skills and traits. Your actual skills and traits will most likely be different. Upon completion of these lists, identify what you believe are your five strongest skills and traits and list them at the bottom of the form. You will also list these five skills and traits in the Assessment Summary Sheet at the end of this chapter.

| Knowledge-based Skills | Transferable Skills | Personal Traits |
| --- | --- | --- |
| Budgeting | Writing Skills | Achievement Oriented |
| Management | Computer Skills | Loyal |
| Facilities Management | Analytical skills | Friendly |
| Media Relations | Time Management | Outgoing |
| Marketing | Management | Honest |
| Sales | Budgeting | Well organized |
| Planning skills | | |

## Top Five Skills and Traits

1. Honesty
2. Good Manager
3. 
4. 
5. 

Form 1.3

## List of Skills

The third assessment is the *List of Skills* exercise. It was
designed using the four groups of Foundation Skills that
Lawrence K. Jones outlined on the website "The Career Key".[13]
Jones outlined 17 Foundation Skills that were grouped into four
major categories: Basic Skills, Thinking Skills, People Skills,
and Personal Qualities. These four types of foundation skills are
the basis for the *List of Skills* exercise. The number of skills has
been expanded to 50, but they remain within these four distinct
groups.

As you begin this exercise, place a checkmark by each of the
skills that you possess. This should help you to better
understand the qualities you possess and how you can be an
asset to a potential future employer. Upon completion of this
exercise, list your top five skills in the *Assessment Summary
Sheet* at the end of this chapter.

# List of Skills

**Directions:** Place a checkmark by each of the skills you possess. List your top five skills in the Assessment Summary Sheet at the end of the chapter.

Basic Skills
___Reading
___Research
___Computer
___Writing
___Detail Oriented
___Communication
___Spelling
___Math
___Speaking
___Listening

People Skills
___Managing
___Teaching
___Persuasion
___Friendliness
___Respect for Feelings
___Assertion
___Negotiation
___Conflict Resolution
___Selling
___Leading
___Servicing
___Motivation
___Honesty
___Teamwork
___Respect for Diversity
___Counseling Skills

Personal Qualities
___Self-Confident
___Positive Thinking
___Goal Oriented
___Honest
___Hard Working
___Do quality work
___Integrity
___Responsible
___Common Sense
___Creative
___Dependable
___Loyal
___Self-Motivated
___Adaptable
___Professional
___Willingness to Learn

Thinking Skills
___Creative Thinking
___Problem-Solving Skills
___Decision Making Skills
___Visualization
___Reasoning
___Analyzing
___Planning
___Organizing

Form 1.4

## Motivated Strengths and Enjoyable Activities Exercise

The fourth assessment tool is the *Motivated Strengths and Enjoyable Activities Exercise*. It is based on the work of career development specialist Bernard Haldane. In his book, Career Satisfaction and Success, Haldane outlined a method for people to identify their strengths or motivated skills through an assessment known as the System to Identify Motivated Skills (SIMS).[14] Haldane referred to the combination of a person's talents, and the motivation to use these talents, as motivated skills.

In the SIMS exercise, a person would identify their strengths and skills by identifying and studying the achievements they have obtained throughout their life. By analyzing the skills, they have used to accomplish their achievements, a person would begin to see a pattern emerge as to which skills they consistently used to achieve their successes. The theory is that if a person could identify the skills and strengths that they used to achieve past successes, they could identify a career that uses these types of skills. And if a person were able to use these types of skills in their future job, a person would be successful in their career.

The SIMS exercise would have you answer seven questions in an attempt to identify your top ten achievements. These questions would have you describe the achievement, which activities you enjoyed the most, and then rank the achievements by which ones you believed were the most important in your life.[15]

Kate Wendleton had a similar assessment known as the Seven Stories Exercise. In this assessment, a person would identify the experiences in their life that they "enjoyed doing and also did well."[16] Once they had identified approximately 25 experiences, they would then narrow these experiences to their top seven (from a sense of accomplishment perspective). They would then write a story that describes each of these seven accomplishments, and analyze each story to see if there is a pattern of the skills they used, and enjoyed using, during each of these experiences.[17]

The Motivated Strengths and Enjoyable Activities Exercise is similar to these assessments in that it attempts to identify the skills or strengths that you possess, and what activities you enjoy. The theory is that if a person can identify their strengths, and the activities that they enjoy, they will then be able to select a career in college sports that best fits their talents and interests. This in turn will lead to a successful and enjoyable career. To identify your motivated strengths, complete the following exercise and list your top five skills and enjoyable activities at the end of the assessment, and also on the *Assessment Summary Sheet.*

## The Motivated Strengths and Enjoyable Activities Exercise

**Directions:** This exercise is designed to help you identify the skills and talents that you are good at and also that you enjoy doing. Complete each step of the exercise and list your top five skills and abilities both at the end of this exercise and also in the Assessment Summary Sheet.

**Step 1:** On a piece of paper, make a list of your top 5-10 accomplishments, achievements, or enjoyable activities from the following five areas of your life – childhood, middle school, high school, college, and work life. This list might take an hour or even a couple of days to develop. Below are examples of what these accomplishments, achievements, or activities might resemble.

### Childhood

Won a Blue Ribbon at the County Fair

Took a field trip to the Space Museum

Won a bike in a Salmon Fishing Derby

Attended Summer Basketball Camp

### Middle School

Made the Jr. High Football Team

Attended the LA Summer Olympics

Participated in the school play

Got an "A" in Math

Won Award for President's Physical Fitness

**High School**

Basketball team played in the state tournament

Won the basketball team's most improved award

Was the Editor of the school newspaper

Made the winning basket in a playoff game

Received a scholarship to attend college

**College**

Played college basketball

Was a vice president of my fraternity

Graduated from college

Started a fundraising event

**Work Life**

Married my wife

Became a head coach

Team won the conference championship

Keynote speaker at the convention

Was responsible for fund raising project

27 of 28 players have graduated

**Step 2:** Once you have a comprehensive list, rank these accomplishments, achievements, or activities for your level of satisfaction or enjoyment.

**Step 3:** Take your top six accomplishments and/or achievements and write a descriptive story about the situation. As you describe the situation and your accomplishments, make sure that you list the skills and abilities that you have used in order to make the outcome a success. Also describe what it was about the experience that was enjoyable.

**Step 4:** After identifying the skills and abilities that were used in each of the individual stories, look to see if there are common skills or abilities used throughout each of the successes. Also, look to see if there were common enjoyable experiences within each of the six stories.

**Step 5:** Take these common skills and experiences and list them below as your motivated strengths. Also list these motivated strengths on the *Assessment Summary Sheet* at the end of this chapter.

_____       _____

_____       _____

_____

**Step 6:** As you review and analyze each of your six stories, list the three types of activities that you enjoyed the most. List these activities below and also on the *Assessment Summary Sheet* at the end of this chapter

_____       _____

_____

Form 1.5

Once you have identified your motivated strengths, and your enjoyable experiences, list them in the *Assessment Summary Sheet* at the end of this chapter. Your skills, abilities, strengths, and talents will be used later in the job search process when you create your cover letter, develop your *Personal Sales Pitch*, and in how you answer interview questions.

## Types of Testing

The four assessment exercises that were outlined in this chapter are by no means the only assessment tools that can assist you in analyzing your skills, strengths, and traits. Many more assessments are available if you still feel that you need more information about yourself. These assessments can include two types of tests – personality tests and career tests. Typically, either a licensed psychologist or a licensed counselor is needed to conduct a personality test. Personality tests tend to measure a wide variety of personality traits, whereas career tests tend to measure a person's aptitude for a skill or a particular interest.

### Personality Tests

There are a wide variety of personality tests available, and they measure a wide variety of personality traits. These include, but are not limited to, such traits as assertiveness, sales aptitude, self-esteem, charisma, social anxiety, and empathy. These personality tests can be used to determine if a person fits the prototype of someone who has the necessary skills to perform a particular job. Three of the better-known personality tests are the Keirsey Temperament Sorter, the Myers and Briggs Type Indicator, and the Jung Typology Test.

**The Keirsey Temperament Sorter** – The Keirsey Temperament Sorter is a test that people can take on the Internet and it measures four temperaments of a person. Temperament is defined as "a configuration of observable personality traits, such as habits of communication, patterns of action, and sets of characteristic attitudes, values, and talents."[18] Taking this test could be helpful in attempting to determine what type of job, or even career, is right for you.

**Myers and Briggs Type Indicator** – Meyers and Briggs is probably the most well-known personality test. This test identifies and describes 16 personality types based upon the preferences of the person taking the test.[19] Again, results of the test can help a person determine what type of a career or job best fits their personality. This test can also be administered over the Internet.

**Jung Typology Test** – The Jung Typology Test can also be administrated over the Internet. It measures a person's strengths and personality type. The test is based on Carl Jung and Isabel-Myers-Briggs typological approach to personality. The results of the test can assist a person in assessing their strengths, and covers such areas as leadership and career development.[20]

## Career Tests

Career tests usually measure a person's aptitude for a skill or a particular interest. In essence, career tests attempt to help you figure out which careers would be most satisfying and successful for you. There are several tests to choose from. They can range from testing a person's level of honesty, to their management style, to their skills and interests. In this book, we have provided you with a systematic approach to understanding career development within the world of college sports. This systematic approach will help you to assess your skills, interests, strengths, weaknesses, and career goals.

# Self-Assessment Summary

The *Assessment Summary Sheet* is a summary of all of the information that you gathered from your assessment exercises. This information includes what skills and job responsibilities you like and dislike; your top skills, abilities, strengths, and traits; and what type of jobs correspond with your skills and abilities. Upon gathering this information, you will use it both in your job search materials and in your interviews.

## Assessment Summary Sheet

**Directions:** Fill in the blanks below from the corresponding assessment exercises.

### From Sports Related Occupational Values:

Top 4 Likes_____ Top 4 Dislikes_____

_____ _____

_____ _____

_____ _____

    **Jobs of Interest:**_____ _____ _____

### From Skills and Traits Assessment

List top five skills and traits _____

_____

_____

_____

_____

### From List of Skills

List top five skills and abilities _____

_____

_____

_____

_____

### From The Motivated Strengths and Enjoyable Activities Exercise

List Your Top Five Skills and Abilities

List Your Top Three Enjoyable Activities

_____     _____

_____     _____

_____     _____

_____

_____

Form 1.6

# Action Steps

The purpose of this chapter was to help you to identify the skills, abilities, strengths, and traits that you possess. As you begin to build your Workbook Binder, you will want to include the results of your assessments into the first section of the binder.

**Action Step** – Place the results of the four assessments from this chapter in the first section of your Workbook Binder. The four assessments include:

- *Sports-Related Occupational Values Assessment* (Form 1.2)
- *Skills and Traits Assessment* (Form 1.3)
- *List of Skills* (Form 1.4)
- *Motivated Strengths and Enjoyable Activities Exercise* (Form 1.5)

**Action Step** – Place the *Assessment Summary Sheet* from this chapter in the first section of your Workbook Binder (Form 1.6).

*CHAPTER 5*

# Identifying Your Dream Job

I n the previous chapter you outlined your strengths and weaknesses, your motivated skills and abilities, and identified the types of jobs that initially seem right for you. In this chapter, you will take these skills and further develop your career path by identifying your ultimate or "dream" job and the steps that you will need to take to position yourself for this ultimate job.

After you have identified your ultimate or "dream" job, you will then break down your career into the steps that are needed in order to reach this "dream" position. A step-by-step plan will be established, and you will have identified your dream job and the steps that are needed in order to reach your career goals.

Once you have established your career path, you will then want to identify the organizations that are included in the first step of the career process. These organizations will be your target market for your upcoming job search. A target market is an organized listing of the colleges or organizations that meet the criteria that you have established for your search, such as the region of the country in which you want to live, the type of institution you want to work for, and/or the level of competition at which they compete. After identifying your target market, the next step will be for you to identify whom the appropriate person is to contact at each of the institutions.

## Identifying Your Dream Job

By now you probably know what type of job you want within college sports. If so, move ahead to the next section and begin work on your *Career Planning Guide*. For those who are not quite sure what type of job you want, it is recommended that you do two things. The first is to conduct an informational interview with someone who is employed in the type of job you think you might want. This is a technique that many companies utilize to help the jobseeker better understand the industry. For example, if a person wanted to become an insurance agent for State Farm Insurance, they are asked to conduct an informational interview with an established agent and to write a report on their findings. This is a great exercise that provides the prospective agent with a more in-depth understanding of the industry. By using this technique, you will become more familiar with the "in's and out's" of the world of college sports.

The second recommendation is for you to get an entry-level job within college sports. When you are working in the industry, you will become exposed to many of the aspects of that industry. This includes which periodicals to read, what are the current issues facing the industry, and what are the duties a person actually performs on a daily basis. If you are a current student, try to get a job within the recreation or athletics department. If you are in the working world and are wanting to make a transition into college sports, see if you can work part-time (even as a volunteer) at events such as home athletic contests or recreational activities. This experience will help you to better understand the nature of the industry, it will look great on a resume, and it will start to build your network.

To begin your career planning process, you will want to complete the *Career Planning Guide* that is outlined in the next section. If you are unsure as to what your ultimate job is within college sports, you will want to focus on identifying your first job within the industry. To do this, skip steps one and two, and move to the 2-year career goal in step three. If you are an out-going and extroverted person, you will probably want to list one of the external areas within athletics as your 2-year goal. This could include marketing, fund raising, or sports information. If you are more of an introverted person, you will probably want to list one of the internal areas within athletics as your 2-year career goal. This could include compliance, business management, or academic advising. This 2-year goal will be a starting point for you until you receive the experience necessary to determine your career goals within the industry. Therefore, the next step in the job search process is to complete the *Career Planning Guide* that follows this section. It will have you map out, step-by-step, the jobs that will ultimately lead to your "dream" job.

## Career Planning Guide

The purpose of the *Career Planning Guide* is for you to create a step-by-step plan of the type of jobs you should be pursuing as intermediary steps toward your ultimate or "dream" job. You will want to establish strategies that you could use to position yourself for when these intermediary jobs become available.

The *Career Planning Guide* will take some real thought and introspection. If you are not sure what type of position you want for your ultimate job, then you will want to complete as much of the worksheet as you can. For instance, you might know that you want to live in a particular region, even if you do not have an ultimate job in mind. That is okay. Maybe your ultimate job is to have a management type position in the region where you want to live. If this is your situation, start your planning guide by identifying an organization or organizations where you would want to work. List these organizations and the title of "management" in step one of the planning guide. Now, working backwards complete steps two, three, and four.

For those people who are extremely focused on their dream job, this exercise might take a matter of minutes. For those who do not know what their ultimate job is, it could take hours or even days to make sense of this. If this is your situation, complete as much of the guide as you can and keep coming back to the guide, completing a little here and some there. Eventually, the fog will begin to lift and you will see a well laid out plan develop.

## Step-by-Step

The first step in the *Career Planning Guide* is to identify and combine six items – the type of position you are seeking, the industry you want to pursue, the type of institution, the level of competition, the region where you want to live, and the size of community where you want to live. List these items in step one of the planning guide.

As you begin to identify these criteria, a clear picture will begin to come into focus. For example, if you want to be an athletic director at the NCAA Division I level, in the Pacific Northwest, and the size of the community does not matter, your dream job is narrowed to 12 institutions. These universities include the University of Washington, Washington State University, Eastern Washington University, Gonzaga University, Seattle University, Boise State University, University of Idaho, Idaho State University, Portland State University, University of Portland, University of Oregon, and Oregon State University.

However, if you add the criteria of wanting to live in a metropolitan community, your target is narrowed to seven institutions – Washington, Gonzaga, Seattle, Boise State, Portland State, Portland, and Oregon. If you want to further narrow (segment) it down by only including those institutions in a metropolitan area that offer major college football programs (Bowl Championship Subdivision), then you have narrowed your target to Washington, Oregon, and Boise State.

Once you have determined your dream job, you will then begin to do the research to uncover what particular steps are necessary and logical to eventually achieve that dream job. For example, what type of skills and education are needed for this position? Also, what are the typical types of positions that could eventually lead to your dream job? If your goal is to become an athletic director, the job that immediately precedes this position could be an associate athletic director at the same (or higher) level of competition, or an athletic director from a lower level of competition. If your dream job is to be an athletic director at a private institution, then you will probably want to gain experience as an associate athletic director at a similar type institution. In other words, you are not just gaining experience; you are gaining experience at an institution that helps you to be a good fit at the institution of your dream job.

The following schematic shows a potential flow chart of how a person might map out their career on a job-by-job basis that will eventually lead to that ultimate job of being an athletic director.

Assistant Marketing Director – *Leading to Marketing Director*

↓

Marketing Director – *Job leading to Assistant AD Job*

↓

Assistant Athletic Director – *Job leading to Associate AD Job*

↓

Associate Athletic Director – *Job leading to the Dream Job*

↓

Athletic Director – *Dream Job*

This progression could easily be for a head coaching position as well. The dream job might be as a Division I head coach in basketball. The job leading to the head coaching position might be a lower level (Division) head coach or more likely a higher-level assistant coach. This process of positioning yourself would continue to flow down the chart until you reach the position you are in now, or it could lead to an entry-level position such as a graduate assistant coach.

With each step along the way you are strategically positioning yourself for your next job. You will want to make sure that you remain focused on doing a great job at your current position, while also preparing yourself for what is needed for your next position. Preparation for that next position could include such items as:

- Becoming a better public speaker – develop a plan that might include taking a course or hiring a professional speech coach.

- Obtaining the skills necessary to do the next job in the progression, possibly an accounting course, taking a writing course, etc.

- What experiences do you need to be qualified for your ultimate job? This will probably include becoming an expert in your particular field, such as marketing, fund raising, coaching football, etc. Study all that you can about your field. Join the national association for your industry. Try to become published in the association's journal. Become a speaker at the national convention.

- Who do you need to network with in order to be in a position to be hired for that next job when it becomes available?

However, if you are attempting just to enter the sports profession, your goal might be to get your first job in the industry. In this situation, skip steps one and two in the planning guide and focus on your 2-year career goal. Identify your 2-year goal in step three as an entry-level position. Utilize the various strategies in step four to gain your entry position. Once you are employed in the profession, you will want to complete the Career Planning Guide in its entirety.

# Career Planning Guide
## Step-by-Step Career Worksheet

**Directions:** Complete the following four steps to identify your long-term career goal (dream job), and the steps it will take to position you for this position.

### Step 1: What is Your Dream Job?
(Complete the criteria that are applicable to you)

Type of Position (i.e. athletic director)_____

Industry (i.e. Sports Administration, Recreation, Coaching)_____

_____

Type of Institution (Public/Private, 2-year/4-year)_____

Level of Competition_____

Where you want to live (region)_____

Size of Community_____

*Research which institutions meet the above criteria and list the type of institution and the type of job that would be your "Dream Job".*

**What is your ultimate or Dream Job?** _____
(e.g. Athletic Director in a Pac-12 Conference school)

### Step 2: How to Get There

As you plan for your dream job, research what type of education, experience, and skills you will need in order to be hired for this position. Answer the following questions:

What educational training is needed for attaining your dream job? (e.g. a master's degree)

_____

What experience is necessary for attaining your dream job? (e.g. previous coaching experience)

_____

What skills are necessary for attaining your dream job? (e.g. budgeting, public speaking)_____

# Career Planning Guide
## (Continued)

### Step 3: Positioning Yourself

Working backwards, what type of positions will lead to your dream job? The assumption is that you are just beginning your career and that your dream job is approximately 10-15 years into the future. This also assumes that it will take approximately four career moves before you reach your dream job. These assumptions will change depending upon where you currently are in your career. Therefore, it might only take two moves instead of four. With this in mind, work backwards from your "dream" situation in step one, and identify what the logical job would be that could lead to your career goal. This is your "One-Position Removed" job. List this position on the first line below. Continue on with this format and identify the type of employment that would lead to your one-position removed job. This is your "Two-Positions Removed" job. List this on the second line below. Complete this process by identifying your 2-Year Career Goal. Your 2-year goal should lead to your "Two-Positions Removed" job. List your 2-year career goal on the third line in step three.

**One-Position Removed** _____
(This is the job that will position you for your ultimate career goal. During your time in this position, you should be focusing on gaining the proper experiences that will lead to your ultimate goal, and also focusing on networking.)

**Two-Positions Removed**_____
(This job should position you to be hired for your "One-Position Removed" job. During your time in this position you should focus on acquiring the skills and experiences that will be necessary to be hired for your next job.)

**2-Year Career Goal**_____
(This job should position you to be hired for the job that is two steps removed from your "dream" job. During your time in this job what do you need to do to put yourself in a position to reach your two-positions removed job? Do you need to return to school and get a master's degree? Do you need to get experience in the industry? What skills can you develop? Networking is necessary for advancement.)

**Career Planning Guide**
(Continued)

**Step 4: Current Situation**

Current Position_____

**Strategies to use to be hired into your next position within two years (check all that are appropriate):**
To achieve your 2-year career goal, do you need to:

_____Reposition yourself within the industry

_____Obtain an entry level Job

_____Stay in your current position and begin a networking plan

**Additional strategies:**
_____Develop a networking Plan (Refer to Chapter 9)

_____Volunteer to gain experience

_____Attend Graduate/Undergraduate School

_____Complete an internship (paid or unpaid)

_____Shadow someone within the industry (a day-in-the-life)

_____Schedule an informational interview

_____Find a mentor who can give you perspective and advice

Form 2.1

# Establishing Your Target Market(s)

Now that you have completed the *Career Planning Guide*, it is time to turn your focus to your next career move. Your next career move will be the job that you want to get within the next two years (Your 2-year career goal). To begin this process, you will want to identify both the type of job that you want and which institutions meet the criteria for your 2-year career goal. Once you have identified the type of job that you want and which institutions you want to work for, you will now have a very focused target market to which you can promote yourself. Therefore, the next step is to identify the job you want and which institutions are in the target market for your 2-year career goal.

As was mentioned previously, a target market is an organized listing of colleges or organizations that meet the criteria that you have established for your search. This can include such segment criteria as the region of the country in which you want to live, the type of institution you want to work for, and/or the level of competition at which they compete.

You will want to start to build your target market by identifying which segment criteria are important to you and which organizations or colleges fit these criteria. You will then focus on the type of job function (e.g. sports information) that interests you. Combine these segment criteria with the job function and you now have identified your target market. For example, if a person wants to pursue public relations in a college or university athletic department within the San Francisco area, they would probably want to look at advancement, marketing, and/or communications positions at UC Berkeley, Stanford, University of San Francisco, Santa Clara, San Jose State, St. Mary's, San Francisco State, California State East Bay, Sonoma State, Academy of Arts, or Notre Dame de Namur. This would be your target market for NCAA Division I and NCAA Division II institutions. If you expanded your target for approximately 100 miles or so, you would also include Sacramento State, UC Davis, Fresno State, University of the Pacific, Chico State, CSU Stanislaus, and CSU Monterey Bay. You would also have the conference offices for The Pac-10, The Big West, the West Coast Conference, and the California Collegiate Athletic Association. As you can see, the broader the criteria, the more institutions that will be within your target market.

The exercise on the following page, *Establishing Your Target Market(s),* is designed to help you determine the target market you will want to focus on during your upcoming job search. By answering the questions within the exercise, a clear set of organizations should be identified. In the example that follows, the form is already completed so as to show you how it might look. In this example, the form was completed by assuming that the person searching for a job wants to work in a sports information office, in an athletic department of a 4-year institution, and within the state of Iowa.

## Establishing Your Target Market(s)

**Directions** – Identify the type of position that you are targeting for your next job, and answer the following five questions to identify the types of institutions where you would want to work.

**Type of Position** – What type of job do you want to pursue for your next job?__**Sports Information**_____
(i.e. Marketing, Fund Raising, Coaching Baseball, Compliance, etc.)

**Identify the Organizations**
1.  What area of college sports (type of sports organization) do you want to pursue?

____X_Intercollegiate Athletics
_____Recreational Sports
_____Coaching (List the sport)
_____Administration
_____Affiliated Associations
_____Other _____

2.  What type of institution do you want to work for?

_____State Supported
_____Private
_____2-year College
___X_4-year College

3.  The level of competition:

___X_NCAA Division I
___X_NCAA Division II
____X_NCAA Division III
___X_NAIA
_____NJCAA
_____Other

3. Where do you want to live and work (geographic area)?
__State of Iowa__

4. What size of the community do you want to live in (i.e.
metropolitan, rural, etc.)?
__Does Not Matter__

Form 3.1

# Identifying Institutions in Your Target Market

As you begin to identify your target market, remember that you
could have several markets depending upon your skills and the
type of positions or industries that you are attempting to enter.
For example, the first target market could be marketing positions
within all Division I universities in the Midwest. A second target
market could be fund raising positions within small colleges in
the State of Iowa. Both are external type positions, but also, both
are in different target markets.

Your target market does not have to be by industry. For
example, your criteria could be searching for a particular type of
job within a certain location – such as a marketing position in
Des Moines Iowa. In this case, your focus crosses all types of
industries, but remains on a certain position in a certain
geographical location. In this situation, your target market will
be a marketing position in Des Moines, Iowa.

A second target market could be marketing positions in a
different location such as nearby Omaha, Nebraska or Cedar
Rapids, Iowa. Your first target market will probably consume
the majority of your job search efforts, but a secondary target
could be a good backup. Regardless of the market or markets, to
conduct a successful search in the sports industry you will want
to include all colleges or organizations that meet the criteria you
have established for your target market.

The form that follows will help you to focus your search on a certain target market. Complete the form by identifying the target market, and the type of position in which you are searching. Make copies of this form if you have two or more target markets. The institutions that you list on this worksheet will be the focus for your search.

## Institutions Within Your Target Market

**Directions:** Fill-in the information below, regarding the target market that you plan to pursue and the type position. Next by doing some research and investigating, list the companies or colleges that match your target market. Depending on your focus, you might have more than one target market. In searching for a list of companies and their contacts, use a telephone book, an Internet search (e.g. NCAA.org), industry directories (e.g. The College Blue Book, NACDA Directory), or consult with a librarian. Below is a sample of the institutions within the target market.

Target Market: College Athletic Departments in Iowa   Date_____

Position/Function:  Sports Information_____

Institutions:

| | |
|---|---|
| University of Iowa | Dordt College |
| Iowa State University | University of Dubuque |
| University of Northern Iowa | Grinnell College |
| Drake University | Luther College |
| Upper Iowa University | Northwestern College |
| Briar Cliff University | Wartburg College |

 (Continue with all Iowa colleges)

Form 3.2

# Target Market Contact List

Upon completion of the worksheet, *Institutions Within Your Target Market*, it is time to gain a greater focus for each organization that you have identified. To gain this focus, you will complete the *Target Market Contact List*. This form has you identify specifics about each institution within your target market – the name of the institution, the contact person, his/her telephone number, their address, and any notes that will help you personalize yourself with the contact person or the company.

The best way to identify this information is through the Internet. Typically, a company's webpage is more current and accurate then an industry directory. The directory is good for identifying organizations within an industry and their corresponding information such as a telephone number or their address. But the Internet is best for identifying who holds what position and possibly even a direct telephone number or e-mail address.

Complete the *Target Market Contact List* worksheet by listing each of the organizations within your target market. Upon completion of this form, you will add this worksheet to the third section within your binder.

# Target Market Contact List

**Directions:** Use this worksheet to organize the information for each organization within your target market. This includes the name of the company, the contact person, their telephone number, address, e-mail address, and any pertinent notes about the contact person or the organization.

Target: <u>Sports Information - Iowa</u>          Date_____

1. **Name of Institution**          **Contact Person**
   University of Iowa              List Name of SID
   402 Carver-Hawkeye Arena        List Phone #_____
   Iowa City, IA  52242            E-mail _____

   **Notes**
   <u>Note any openings if available or significant findings</u>
   _____

2. **Name of Institution**          **Contact Person**
   Iowa State University          List Name of SID
   1800 S. Fourth, Jacobson Bldg.  List Phone #_____
   Ames, IA  50011                E-mail _____

   **Notes**
   _____
   _____

3. **Name of Institution**          **Contact Person**
   Univ. of Northern Iowa         List Name of SID
   UNI Dome                       List Phone #_____
   Cedar Falls, IA  50614         E-mail _____

   **Notes**
   _____
   _____

*Continue to list all of the institutions within your target market*

Form 3.3

# Action Steps

This chapter is designed to help you identify your dream job and how to position yourself along the way so you can establish a step-by-step plan for achieving this dream. Below are four action steps. Complete each action step and include them in your Worksheet Binder.

**Action Step** – Complete your *Career Planning Guide* by following the four steps that are outlined in the worksheet. Once completed, place your *Career Planning Guide* (Form 2.1) in Section Two of your Workbook Binder.

**Action Step** – Next, develop your target market by completing the *Establishing Your Target Market(s)* form (Form 3.1). This worksheet asks you to list the type of job that you are pursuing, and has you answer five questions that will help you to identify the type of organizations that you will be targeting. This form will be the front page in Section Three of your Worksheet Binder.

**Action Step** – The third action step in this chapter is for you to complete the form *Institutions Within Your Target Market* (Form 3.2) and to place it as the second page in third section of your binder.

**Action Step** – The final action step in this chapter is for you to complete the *Target Market Contact List* (Form 3.3) for each organization that you are targeting. Place this form(s) behind the first two forms in Section Three of your binder.

## CHAPTER 6

---

# Developing Your Promotional Materials

I n the previous chapter you identified the colleges or organizations where you would want to work. Now you will want to create a strategy that will help you to network into or sell yourself to these organizations.

The initial step in creating a strategy for your job search is to develop your promotional materials. Promotional materials are the items that you will use to promote and sell yourself to potential employers. These items include your resume, your cover letter, your list of references, and your sales pitch. If constructed properly, these items will increase the chances that you will get an interview. However, if your promotional items are not good, you are almost guaranteed not to get an interview.

As you begin to put your promotional materials together, the first item that you will need to develop is your resume. A resume is a summary of a person's education, work experience, and professional qualifications. There are several styles of resumes a person can use. This book will provide you with the style of resume that is typically found to be the most successful in securing jobs within the world of college sports.

The next step is to create your *Personal Sales Pitch*. The *Personal Sales Pitch* is the foundation for selling yourself in letters and in interviews. Your sales pitch should include a summary of your resume, your skills and abilities, and your current situation. Once completed, these three summaries will flow together for a pitch that you can effectively use to sell yourself.

The third item is to create a captivating cover letter. The objective of the cover letter is to entice the person who is reading the letter into wanting to read the accompanying resume. If the cover letter is poor, the resume might not be read. If a resume is sent without a cover letter, the resume most likely will not be read. The cover letter and the resume need to support and enhance one another, thus making your application that much stronger.

Another way to enhance your resume and cover letter is to properly format them. Using an appropriate font with the right touch of bold, underlining, and italics can make the letter and resume pop out and grab the reader's attention. However, using the wrong font, or over-using bold, underlining, or italics, will turn the reader off and your resume goes into the "no thanks" pile.

The final step in your initial phase of creating a strategy for a job search is to choose the proper people for references. You will want to select the people who will best support your application for a particular position. They should be able to sell you to the potential employer. Not every friend or former employer will be a great reference for every position. This is an often over looked aspect of the job search process. Do not fall into this trap. Carefully select each of your references.

Finally, many coaches and athletic administrators want to out-work their opponents. This is the very nature of the profession. With this type of work ethic, many of these people want to put together another type of promotional piece to help sell themselves to potential employers. This can be a good idea if done properly. The applicant wants the potential employer to be interested in them, but without seeming desperate. Too many e-mails, letters, or telephone calls can turn-off the hiring manager. Therefore, any additional promotional piece is usually best used during the interview phase of the process. Instead of additional materials to help you get that initial interview, use a few (not too many) properly placed telephone calls from people who can influence the hiring manager. The caller needs to be either a friend/colleague of the hiring manager, or in a respected position within the industry.

## Constructing Your Resume

The purpose of a resume is to show the hiring manager that you meet the qualifications for the position. Your resume should be easy to read and it should sell you. In my experience, most employers will initially spend between 10-20 seconds looking at a resume. Therefore, it is important that your resume catches the employer's attention so that they spend more time looking at you and your resume.

Many people will tell you that a resume should be one to two pages in length at a maximum. This is somewhat of a misnomer. A resume needs to be long enough to show your experiences and accomplishments, but short enough that a potential employer will read it. As a person advances in their career, their resume will grow in length. A typical resume will range in length from one page for someone just graduating from high school or college, to four or five pages for someone with significant experience.

A person's resume should be tailored to the position for which they are applying. This does not mean that you have to change your resume every time you apply for a job, but you might want to highlight a particular experience. Your resume needs to effectively use fonts, bullets, bold, and underlining to get the search committee to see what you want them to see. Further, people naturally view written pages from top of the page and down the left margin. Therefore, these areas need to have your most important information. Writing lengthy sentences and paragraphs is a sure-fire way to lose the readers interest and they usually will not continue reading the resume.

The paper that you print your resume on needs to be high quality – usually 24 lb., 100% cotton, white or light in color resume paper. Most office supply stores and copy stores have the correct paper. Remember, the hiring manager will only scan the resume, and the appearance of the resume speaks volumes about who you are. This is the reason mailing your resume – not faxing or e-mailing – is preferred. By mailing your resume you can control the way it looks, and you can control the type of paper it is printed on. If you were to fax a resume, the fax might not print the resume as you intended, and it most certainly will be on the wrong type of paper. Similarly, if you did e-mail a resume, it might not come across on the hiring manager's printer as it did on your printer. To help safeguard this, you should save your resume in a PDF format (instead a Word document) and attach it to your e-mail. If your faxed or e-mailed resume is not completely right, a search committee might not look at your resume with as much interest in comparison to the resumes of the other applicants.

These suggestions and recommendations might seem a little petty, but remember, a resume is your first impression. Put yourself into the shoes of the hiring manager. Do you want to hire someone who is extremely professional and detail oriented, or someone who is average and does not care about quality control and professionalism? The hiring manager did not get to his/her level by not caring about details. Therefore, if you really want the job, sell yourself to them. Be extremely professional in developing your promotional materials. Make sure that the appearance of your promotional materials looks good and that they are error free. Do not settle for "it's okay".

# Mark DaFort

412 South 2nd Street
Irondale, WA 98339
(321) 123-5432
E-mail: markd@xxx.com

## EDUCATION:

**Southern Illinois University**
**M.S. in Education,** 1996
Concentration: Sports Management
Thesis: Communication Styles in NCAA Athletic Departments

**Oregon State University**
**Bachelor of Arts in Communications,** 1994
Concentration: Sports Writing

## WORK EXPERIENCE:

**SPORTS INFORMATION DIRECTOR**
Southwest Washington College, NCAA Division II
(2004 – Current) Irondale, Washington

**Achievements:**
- Received CoSIDA Award – Best Media Guide, Best Design for Promotional Brochures
- Responsible for writing and publishing media guides
- Responsible for maintaining game statistics
- Supervised sports information interns
- Produced all press releases
- Responsible for website design and content
- Sold game program advertising
- Responsible for press conferences

**ASSISTANT SPORTS INFORMATION DIRECTOR**
Idaho State University, NCAA Division I
Big Sky Conference
(1997 – 2004) Pocatello, Idaho

**Achievements:**
- Developed new website
- Produced webcasts for basketball games
- Produced livestats for basketball games
- Responsible for reporting of women's basketball and track
- Developed media guides

**SPORTS INFORMATION INTERN**
Briar Cliff College, NAIA
(1996 – 1997)  Sioux City, Iowa
* Assisted in game management
* Photographer for basketball games
* Experience working with "live stats" software
* Scorekeeper for baseball games
* Wrote press releases for baseball and softball

**GRADUATE ASSISTANT**
Southern Illinois University, NCAA Division I Missouri Valley Conference
(1995 – 1996)  Carbondale, IL
* Wrote press releases for cross country
* Assisted with basketball game management
* Assisted with press conferences
* Experience working with "live stats" software

**STUDENT ASSISTANT**
Oregon State University
  (1990 – 1994)  Corvallis, OR
* Assisted with press releases
* Spotter at basketball games
* Assisted with press conferences

PROFESSIONAL ACTIVITIES:

Member CoSIDA – 9-year member
Worked with NCAA Regional Basketball Tournament – 2006

# Analyzing the Above Resume

Below is an analysis of the resume that is highlighted above. This section will discuss the above resume by its appearance, by its format, and by the fonts that are being used. Each section of the resume is then discussed in greater detail. These sections include the personal information that is listed on the resume, the use of an objective, how to list your education and experience, and the listing of any professional activities that you are associated with or publications that you have authored.

## Format and Appearance

The format and appearance of your resume is critically important. Since the hiring manager will spend approximately 20 seconds initially reviewing a resume, you need to create a format for your resume that highlights who you are, and what you have accomplished. You will want to effectively use the space on the resume so that the hiring manager can scan your resume and know who you are and what you have done. Therefore, the margins should be no less than one inch on all four sides. In addition, you will want to use bulleted items, short statements, and occasionally a sentence to describe your skills and experiences. Written paragraphs are not as effective.

In the sample resume, the top and bottom margins are 1" while the left and right margins are 1.25". People read left-to-right, but they scan top to left. Therefore, it is important to have your name at the top of the resume, and aligned either in the center or to the left. Since people scan down the left side of a document, it is important that your headings, experiences, and accomplishments are listed on the left side of the resume.

## The Font

The font and font size are also critically important. Typically, a 12-point font size and a conservative (and legible) font such as "Times" are used. If you are applying for a position that is creative in nature, you might want to, or need to, use something less conservative. This is where a mentor can help you. In our sample resume, 12-point Times is used for the main information, and 14-point Times is used for the headings. Also, the headings are in all capital letters. Certain items are in bold and are the items you want them to notice. Typos and poor grammar can eliminate you from the search. Therefore, always double-check your spelling and always use spell check on your computer.

## Personal Information

The personal information on your resume should only include your name, address, telephone number, and e-mail address. To highlight your name the sample resume has the font size increased to 24-point, and also is underlined by a colorful line (it does not show in the book). This is the only splash of color on the resume and it is used to create a more attractive, eye-catching, promotional tool. The eye will naturally be attracted to the color, which underlines (highlights) your name. The address, telephone number, and e-mail address are a smaller font, 10-point. The reason for this is if the hiring manager wants to find out how to contact the applicant, it is available to him/her without distracting from the highlights I want them to see.

## Objective

An objective can be used, but is not required on the resume. Typically, if someone is applying for a job in the industry in which they are currently working, they probably do not need an objective. However, if a person is changing industries, or is a recent graduate, an objective is probably warranted. If an objective is used, it should be located after the personal information but before the education. It should be in 12-point and in the same font (e.g. Times) as the body of the resume.

## Education

If you have a college degree(s), list the highest degree first and do not include your high school diploma. However, if you do not have a college degree, you will want to list your high school diploma. In our sample resume, both the college and the degree obtained are bolded. In intercollegiate athletics, these are important items and you want the hiring manager to know where you went to school and what type of degree you earned.

## Experience

List each of your applicable jobs by most recent position first. You will want to list each of your positions by title, institution, dates of employment, and your achievements. The title of your position should be listed in bold. This is so the hiring manager can scan your resume and see what type of experience you have. He/she will then look to see where you have worked and for how long. Make sure that your dates of employment coincide so that it does not appear that you were out of work at any time. However, if you were unemployed at some point, do not try to hide something by falsifying dates. Instead, list the accurate dates in years, such as "1999-2003". Using this format, instead of listing months and years, you will help to possibly defuse any questions about your unemployment.

Whether you describe your period of employment in years, or by month and year, make sure that you are consistent by listing it the same way for each position. If you were unemployed for a time, be prepared to answer any questions that might arise about the unemployed period. Finally, in order to make your accomplishments easy to read, you should bullet each achievement. This too, makes it easy for the hiring manager to scan your resume and see what you have accomplished.

## Professional Activities

If you are a member of a professional association you should include this on your resume. Since this is a new category, the heading should be in a 14-point font size.

## Publications

If you have published an article, a research study, or a book, you should also include this on your resume with an additional heading. This too would be a new heading and would be in 14-point Times.

# Creating Your Personal Sales Pitch

After completing your resume, you are now ready to create your *Personal Sales Pitch*. The *Personal Sales Pitch* is the foundation for selling yourself. It should be used in all correspondence and in answering interview questions. The *Personal Sales Pitch* has three sections – a summary of your resume; your skills, abilities, and traits; and your current situation. Depending upon the interview question, you can use the pitch in its entirety or you can use just one of the three sections. For example, a search committee might ask you to tell them about yourself. You could respond by using the entire pitch. However, if the committee were to ask you about your experience, you could discuss the first section of the pitch – your resume and accomplishments.

The sales pitch needs to be geared towards the type of organization you are interviewing with, and the type of position you are seeking. You will need to be able to recite your sales pitch clearly and with enthusiasm. It is important that the people on the interviewing committee understand who you are, what your accomplishments are, and that you are a good fit for the position.

The following text describes the three sections of the *Personal Sales Pitch*. This is followed by a worksheet for you to develop your own pitch. Use your *Personal Sales Pitch* when writing your cover letters, and during interviews.

## Summary of Resume

The first section of your personal sales pitch is a summary of your professional life. This should include your education, experience, and accomplishments. Typically, you will only mention your educational degree(s) that are applicable to the position and only if they will help sell you during the interview. You will then want to discuss your experiences that are applicable to the position for which you are applying. Finally, you will want to discuss your top three or four accomplishments.

When combined, this information will be used for questions such as *"What is your experience in working in this industry"*, or *"What is your greatest work accomplishment"*, or *"What are your qualifications?"*. An example of this first section could look like the pitch below.

**Section I - Sample Pitch:** *"I have been in college athletics for over 10 years. This includes Sports Information positions at Southern Illinois University, Oregon State University, Briar Cliff University, and Southwest Washington."*

*"During my five years as Sports Information Director at Southwest Washington I have been responsible for writing and publishing media guides, tabulating statistics for all sports teams, supervising sports information interns, producing all press releases, website design and content, and the sales of game program advertising."*

## Skills, Abilities, and Traits

The second section of your personal sales pitch should be developed from the information on your *Assessment Summary Sheet*. You will want to take your top five or six strengths, skills, abilities and/or traits, and develop a pitch that best describes who you are and what you value. This information will be used to answer questions such as *"What are your strengths"* or *"How would your colleagues describe you"*. An example of this second section could look like the pitch below.

**Section 2 – Sample Pitch:** *"I am a hard worker who is honest, achievement oriented, respectful of others, and I strive to create a department that works together and has a positive work environment."*

## Current Situation

The third section of your personal sales pitch is the conclusion to your pitch and should describe your current situation and how you would fit into their institution. This section of the pitch should be used for questions such as *"Why are you thinking of leave your current position"* or *"What are you looking for in an institution"*. An example of this third section could look like the pitch below.

> **Section 3 – Sample Pitch:** *"Currently I am looking for a job in sports information in my home state of Iowa."*

## The Finalized Personal Sales Pitch

Your finalized personal sales pitch is the combination of all three pitches. Write all three of these presentations in a way so that they flow together and they accurately sell you. This pitch will be the foundation of selling yourself during your search and will be used in your cover letter, networking, and interview sessions. Practice this presentation until it becomes second nature. This should help you be prepared to answer the questions "So tell me about yourself" or "Walk me through your resume." An example of your entire sales pitch could look like the pitch below.

> **Sample Completed Pitch:** *"I have been in college athletics for over 10 years. Currently I am the Sports Information Director at Southwest Washington College where I am responsible for writing and publishing media guides, tabulating statistics for all sports teams, supervising*

*sports information interns, producing all press releases, website design and content, and I sold game program advertising."*

"I am a hard worker who is honest, achievement oriented, respectful of others, good with finances, and I strive to create a department that works together and has a positive work environment."

*"Currently I am looking for a job in sports information in my home state of Iowa."*

# Personal Sales Pitch – Worksheet

On the page that follows is a worksheet that is designed for you to develop your own *Personal Sales Pitch*. Use your resume and creativity to complete the first section. The second section of your pitch is a description of your skills, abilities, and traits that you listed in your *Assessment Summary Sheet* at the end of chapter four. The final section of your sales pitch describes what you are currently doing. Always be positive in writing your pitch. If you are currently unemployed, do not write that you have been unemployed for six months because your boss did not like you. Instead, put a positive spin on it and describe something to the effect that you are looking to move closer to home (if that job is closer to home). However, in your preparations, you will need to be able to explain why you are currently unemployed. Again, keep it as positive as possible. Finally, combine all three of these sections to form your overall *Personal Sales Pitch*. Practice reciting your pitch and be prepared for when you are asked questions such as "Why should we hire you" or "Tell us a little about yourself."

# Personal Sales Pitch
Worksheet

**Directions:** Develop your Personal Sales Pitch by writing a summary of yourself as it pertains to each of the four sections of this worksheet.

## Summary of Resume

The first section of your Personal Sales Pitch is a summary of your resume. It needs to mention your experience and accomplishments and it might also include your education.

*Example: I have been in college athletics for over 20 years. My most recent experience was as athletic director at XYZ University. I inherited an XYZ program that was not successful and was in need of enhanced fund raising.*

*During my five years as athletic director, we turned the program around and had the most successful sports season in the history of XYZ athletics. In addition, we were 4th in the nation in graduation rates, we significantly increased our fund raising, balanced our budget, and established a reserve account.*

Pitch:_____

_____

_____

## Skills, Abilities and Traits

This section should be developed from your *Assessment Summary Sheet.* Simply take your top five or six strengths, skills, abilities and/or traits, and develop a pitch that best describes who you are and what you value.

*Example: I am a hard worker who is honest, achievement oriented, respectful of others, good with finances, and I strive to create a department that works together and has a positive work environment.*

Pitch:_____

_____

## Current Situation

This section is the conclusion to the pitch and should describe your current situation and how you would fit into their institution.

*Example:* Currently I am looking to get back into college athletics at an institution that values my experiences, hard work, and integrity.

Pitch:_____

_____

## Personal Sales Pitch

Your *Personal Sales Pitch* is the combination of all three pitches from above. Write all three pitches in a way so that they flow together and that they accurately describe you.

*Example:*
*I have been in college athletics for over 20 years. My most recent experience was as athletic director at XYZ University. I inherited an XYZ program that was not successful and was in need of enhanced fund raising.*

*During my five years as athletic director, we turned the program around and had the most successful sports season in the history of XYZ athletics. In addition, we were 4th in the nation in graduation rates, we significantly increased our fund raising, balanced our budget, and established a reserve account.*

*I am a hard worker who is honest, achievement oriented, respectful of others, good with finances, and I strive to create a department that works together and has a positive work environment.*

*Currently I am looking to get back into college athletics at an institution that values my experiences, hard work, and integrity.*

Pitch:_____

_____

Form 5.1

# Writing Your Cover Letter

A resume should seldom be delivered without an accompanying cover letter. The cover letter, like your resume, should be viewed as a marketing tool. Its purpose is to sell you, provide insight into you as a person, and show why you are a good fit for the position. The following section describes both the appropriate format to use and the proper appearance in creating your cover letter.

## Format

The format of the cover letter should consist of a heading, the salutation, an introduction, the body of the letter, the closing paragraph, and the complimentary close. Each of these topics is discussed below.

**Heading** – The heading includes your address, the employer's address, and the date. Begin by typing your address at least one inch down from the top of the page. This is followed by the date. Space four times and type the name of the person you are sending the letter to, the title of their position, the name of the employer, and their address.

**Salutation** – The salutation is the proper introduction to the letter. It should include "Dear" and then the person's title and their last name. Always attempt to address the letter to the appropriate person and not "To Whom It May Concern". You will also want to address the person by their proper title (Mr., Ms., Dr.) and their last name. If you cannot find the name of the person that you should send your resume to, address the letter as "Dear Search Committee".

**Opening Paragraph** – The opening paragraph should be short and concise. It is an introduction to the letter and should explain why you are writing this letter "I am applying for the position of . . ." and what you have included in the mailing "Enclosed are my resume and a list of references."

**Body** – The body of the letter needs to sell you. It should explain how you meet the stated qualifications, and what are your skills, abilities, and accomplishments. Show why are you a good fit for the position, and how you will make the department successful.

Your *Personal Sales Pitch* should guide you in developing this part of your letter. The body should be written in one to three paragraphs. Each paragraph should be longer than one sentence but shorter than seven lines.

**Closing Paragraph** – The closing paragraph needs to wrap-up the letter and needs to have a call for action. The wrap-up could reiterate why you are a good fit for the position, or it could reiterate what you would do to bring success to the organization. The call for action could be to encourage the hiring manager to call you. This could read like this "Please feel free to call me at (phone number), I look forward to speaking with you soon."

**The Complimentary Close** – After the closing paragraph, double space and type your complimentary close (e.g. Sincerely) followed by a comma. Space four times and type your name. The space between the close and your name is where you are to sign the letter. Always remember to sign the letter with a black or navy ballpoint pen. Too many times people are eliminated because they forget to sign the letter. Do not make this mistake. If you are sending your materials via e-mail, type your name in the signature space, change the font to a handwriting style (e.g. Handwriting – Dakota), and increase the font size to make it look as if you signed your name.

## Appearance

As you write your cover letter, it is important to know that the purpose of the cover letter is to sell you, and to get the hiring manager to want to read your resume. If the letter is written properly, it will accomplish these objectives. However, if the font is too small (or large), if the writing is poor, if there are typos, or if the letter is boring, you will not accomplish these objectives. The following tips are included below to assist you with creating a quality cover letter.

**Type of paper** – The quality of paper is vitally important. Use a resume type paper that is 24lbs and 100% cotton. The paper can have (does not need to have) a watermarking. A linen paper with 25% cotton is an acceptable substitution. The color should be somewhat conservative such as white or ivory. You will probably want to use the same type of paper for your cover letter as you used with your resume. The reason you will want to use a light color paper is that the resume and cover letter will be copied for each member of the search committee. A copy of a dark colored paper does not copy as well as a lighter color.

**Length** – Be concise but thorough. The letter should be long enough to sell yourself, but not so long that it turns-off the reader. There should not be any fluff in the letter. Try to keep your letter on one page and never go longer than one and a third pages.

**Font** – The font should be readable and somewhat conservative (unless you are applying for an extremely creative position – use good judgment). Times or Times Roman are good fonts to use. Try to stay with a readable "point" such as 12-point. Ten-point is typically too small and 14-point is too large. Do not give the reader any reason not to read your letter and resume.

**Style** – There are four basic styles of business letters: block, semi-block, modified block, and modified semi-block.

- **Block Style** – The entire letter is aligned with a left justification. The margins should be one inch, but can be as much as 1 1/2 inches.

- **Semi-block Style** – Similar to the block style letter, the semi-block letter is aligned with a margin that is justified to the left. The difference between the two styles is that in the semi-block style, each paragraph indented.

- **Modified Block Style** – In the modified block style of letter, the sender's information, the date, and the complementary close are centered. However, the remainder of the letter has a margin that is justified to the left.

- **Modified Semi-block Style** – Like the modified block style, this style has the sender's information, date, and the complementary close centered, and the margins justified to the left. However, in the modified semi-block style, each paragraph is indented.

**Use of bold and underline** – Be conservative with the use of bolding and underlining. These should be used to highlight items that you want the reader to notice. Using too much bolding or underlining is hard to read and it takes away from the items you truly want noticed. Typically, bolding and underlining are used more in a resume and do not appear in the cover letter.

**Typos and grammar** – A simple mistake such as a typo or poor grammar can eliminate you from the pool of applicants. Always use spell check on your computer, and have someone who is good with English double check your letter for possible errors. A second set of eyes typically can catch a mistake that the writer does not always see.

**Envelope** – A matching envelope or large white/manila envelope should be used. A large envelope is preferred because the resume and cover letter are in perfect condition when opened and first read. The address on the front of the envelope needs to be typewritten either directly on the envelope or on labels. The font should be in a legible style such as 12-point Times.

**Key Words** – Many employers will have you submit your cover letter and resume electronically. Because of the large volume of resumes they receive, they will scan your documents for key words to see if you meet the qualifications that they require. Therefore, when writing your cover letter, make sure that you write it to meet the criteria that are listed in the job description within the advertisement.

# Sample Letter

Following this section is a sample letter in the format that is preferred within college sports. As was mentioned previously, the length of the letter should never be longer than one and a third pages. The font needs to be in a conservative type such as Times and needs to be in a legible size such as 12-point.

412 South 2nd Street
Irondale, WA 98339
January 28, 2018


Ms. Sandra Thomas
Director of Athletics
Deception Pass University
210 Welts Hall
Oak Harbor, WA 98277

Dear Ms. Thomas,

In response to your announcement for the position of Sports Information Director, please accept this letter and resume for application. Letters of recommendation have been requested and will be sent directly to you.

I believe that with my combination of experience as a Sports Information Director at the NCAA Division II level, having lived in the region, and my education, I would be a good fit for the Sport's Information position at Deception Pass University. Currently, I am the Sports Information Director at Southwest Washington College. Prior to this, I was the Assistant Sports Information Director at Idaho State University for seven years. My education includes a B.A. in Communications from Oregon State University, and an M.S. in Education from Southern Illinois University.

During my time at Southwest Washington, we have won the CoSIDA award for the best media guides in its classification. Our promotional brochures were also recognized for top design. While at Idaho State, we developed a new website that is easy to navigate and looks great. In fact, during my last year at Idaho State we began providing webcasts of the home basketball games and upgraded our basketball contests with live stats.

As the director of a sports information office, I am a firm believer in providing great service to our external communities. We do this through the use of electronic and print publications, and by providing up-to-date statistics and information prior to each contest and updated immediately after each game. In addition, I am a hard worker who is organized and experienced in all aspects of sports information.

Ms. Thomas, I am excited about this opportunity at Deception Pass University. I know that I would be a good fit for the athletics department because I have the experience and education necessary for this position, and we are from the area. Please let me know if there is any additional information I can provide for you or the search committee. Please feel free to contact me at your convenience. My telephone number is (321) 123-5432. I look forward to visiting with you soon.

Sincerely,

*Mark DaFort*

Mark DaFort

# Selecting Your References

References can make or break your job search. A poor or negative reference will almost always keep you from getting the job. If you have any question in your mind if a reference would be negative or even mediocre, either do not use them or ask them if they feel comfortable in providing an outstanding reference for you. Therefore, select your references wisely.

## Who to Ask to Be a Reference

Whomever you select to be a reference, make sure that they give you a positive recommendation. If at all possible, you will want to list your former supervisors on your reference list. If you know a friend or a colleague of the hiring manager, this too would be a great person to list as a reference. This is like trying to "connect the dots". In other words, who do you know who knows the hiring manager and can influence their decision?

Others who can make good references are people of influence within the profession, professors, business acquaintances, and community leaders. The key is that you select people who are able to provide a great recommendation for you.

## Ask for Their Permission

Before you use somebody's name as a reference, ask for his or her permission. You do not want to blindside them by having them receive a telephone call out-of-the-blue by a potential employer. Your references need to be prepared for when the employer calls, so that they can do a good job of selling you. In addition, when you call a potential reference to ask for their permission, this is a good opportunity to provide them with information about what the employer is looking for in a candidate. It is also a good idea to keep your references aware of how your search is progressing.

## Do Not Burn Them Out

On average, employers ask for three references. If you are applying for several positions at the same time, it might be wise to have five or six different references that you can rotate among your applications. This way the same person will not continue to get bombarded by telephone calls. The last thing you want is for your references to get burned out on being a reference for you. You will also want to utilize your references in a strategic manner. Continue to think with the connecting-the-dot mentality and select references who might have an "in" with the hiring manager.

## Provide Your References with Information

It is good to share information about the employer with your references. You can share this information with them by telephone, but it might be better to e-mail the information to them so that they have the selling points in front of them when the hiring manager calls. Two areas of information that are critical for your references to know are: What the institution is looking for in a candidate, and how you meet the needs of the institution.

## What Are They Looking For?

Do your research and figure out what the institution is looking for in a candidate. You can usually get some of this information by carefully reading the job announcement. Remember, that as an applicant, you should be acting like a consultant, so start asking questions. Review newspaper archives, media guides/press booklets, and ask questions of the people who might have knowledge of the organization.

You will want to look for issues of concern, needs, strengths and weaknesses of the organization. Also, get to know the structure of the organization, and who are the members of the search committee. Investigate the search committee members and familiarize yourself with their background. Can you connect-the-dots with any of these committee members? Did you work with someone in the past who also worked with a member of the committee? Share the highlights of your findings with your references, and let them know how your experiences are a good match to address the issues of the company.

## How Do You Meet Their Needs?

Once you have done your research and know the issues, you can share with your references how your experiences match their needs. This is a good time to use your *Sales Pitch* or a portion of it so you can remind your references of your strengths and skills.

# Follow-up with Your References

Stay in contact with your references and ask each of them to contact you after they have spoken with a potential employer. This will help you to gather more information about the search and the search process. Finally, make sure that you thank your references for their help. These suggestions are discussed in further detail below.

## Have Your References Follow-up with You

Ask your references if they would let you know when they receive a call from a potential employer. This gives you an opportunity to find out more information about the search process and to find out more about the issues facing the organization.

## Thank Them

Your references are key for your job search. Make sure that you properly thank them for helping you with the search. A simple "thank you" at the end of a telephone conversation will help, but a follow-up e-mail is a nice touch. Let them know how much you appreciate them and their support.

## Continue to Stay in Touch with Them

Do not take your references for granted. They should be some of your greatest contacts within your network. Continue to cultivate these relationships. Keep them up-to-date on you and your activities. Send them birthday cards, Christmas cards, interesting news items, or just a note of "hello". Try to keep your name in front of them monthly or even quarterly.

# Sample References Page

Below is an example of a reference page. The format is very simple and it provides the information that the search committee needs in order to contact your references.

---

**REFERENCES:**

Ms. Martha Cutbank
Sports Information Director
Oregon State University
60 Jefferson Street
Corvallis, OR 99019
(609) 765-9876
cutbank@net.com

Ms. Bobbi Francis
Associate Athletic Director
Central Washington University
Ellensburg, WA 98209
(206) 299-4500
francis@cwwu.edu

Mr. Arnold Mackay
Sports Information Director
Southern Illinois University
9116 Western States Blvd.
Carbondale, IL 62401
(921) 442-1958
mackay@siuu.com

---

# Strategically Utilizing Your References

References can make or break your candidacy for a position. It is vitally important that you properly list your references on your reference sheet, and that you only list people who will give you a great recommendation. The suggestions that are listed below will provide you with the proper way to list your references on your reference sheet, and will also provide you with suggestions as to how you can strategically utilize your references in an attempt to influence the search committee.

## Listing References on a Reference Sheet

A list of references typically consists of three people. In the business world, references are usually provided upon request, whereas in academia reference sheets quite often accompany the resume and cover letter. The first line of each reference should list the name of the reference along with their title (Mr., Ms., Dr., etc.). The second line should be the title of the person's position (Vice President, Director of Athletics, etc.). This is followed by the name of the institution, the mailing address, their telephone number, and possibly their e-mail address. Make sure that you only list people who will provide you will a glowing recommendation.

## Strategically Placed Influential Telephone Calls

Sometimes it is helpful to have people of influence call the hiring manager or members of the search committee to recommend you for the position. Strategically placed telephone calls can be used to help you get an interview. However, a telephone call at the right time, by the right person, following the interview can help influence the decision of the committee. This is some of the most strategic parts of the hiring process – who to use as a reference, when to use them, and in what capacity.

## The Use of E-mails

Depending upon the hiring manager and the industry, the use of e-mails can be an effective way to communicate. If you get a feel that the hiring officer does not use or does not like using e-mail, do not use it. However, many people prefer to communicate using e-mail.

## Letters of Recommendation

Letters of recommendation can be a hassle for both the applicant and the writer. Quite often when the employer requires letters of recommendation, they do not get the best applicants to apply because of this hassle. However, if letters are required, then by all means have them sent. If letters are required and you do not want the hassle of having them written and sent, do not apply for the job. Many times, people will apply without sending in the letters of recommendation. Typically, these applications will not be looked at because the application file is not complete. Save yourself the time and do not apply unless you are excited about the position and you are going to submit the letters of recommendation.

# Dealing with A Negative Former Boss

Most people have had a boss that they did not like or get along with. If this is your situation, try not to use this former supervisor within your search process. If you believe that he or she will be negative in their communications with the hiring manager, do not use them. In fact, you need to try to steer them away from this negative former boss. The suggestions below will provide you with some insights as to how to deal with a former boss who would provide a negative recommendation.

## Get A Letter of Recommendation Before You Leave

If you are leaving a company on poor terms with your supervisor, attempt to get a positive letter of recommendation before you resign or leave the organization. If you are being forced out, most employers will write something that is not negative. It might not be a glowing review, but at least it is not negative. Make sure that the letter says what you need it to say before submitting your letter of resignation. This letter can be photo copied and submitted, along with your resume, when applying for jobs. By sending a copy of the letter, this sometimes helps so that the potential employer will not call your former boss for a reference on you.

## Do Not List a Negative Former Boss

Do not list a former boss on your reference sheet if you think that he/she will provide a negative review. Only list people as references who will provide a positive reference for you. If you believe that you need someone as a reference from your previous place of employment, and you do not trust that your former supervisor will provide a positive reference for you, ask a colleague if he or she will agree to be a reference for you. Make sure that this colleague will provide a positive recommendation. If there is not a person at your former place of employment who would provide a positive recommendation for you, try to use other references on your reference sheet in an attempt to steer the search committee away from this negative former boss.

## Use an Employment Reference Checking Company

If you are concerned that your former boss is "bad mouthing" you or giving you a negative review, consider hiring a reference check company to check on your reference. The fee is quite nominal and can answer a lot of questions about if you should be using a certain reference.

## Steer Them Away from Your Supervisor

Similar to a negative former boss, if you suspect that your immediate supervisor is going to give you a negative reference, list a co-worker on your reference sheet instead of your supervisor. Let that co-worker know that you are not using the supervisor and ask if they would consider helping you by being a reference.

# Bringing It Together

Now that you have a good concept on how to write a resume, how to develop your cover letter, and how to build a list of references, you are now ready to keep these three documents together in what is to become your main promotional selling piece. This three-piece promotional packet can be, and should be, used when applying for a job. It should not be used, however, during informational interviews or networking sessions. Be prepared in a networking session to provide your resume upon request. Any list of references should be sent upon request.

## Sending Your Resume

Earlier in the chapter it was mentioned how to properly submit your promotional materials for a job. This is an important part of the application process and is worth repeating. Below are the pluses and minuses of sending your resume through the mail, by fax, or by e-mail.

### Envelope

A matching envelope or large white/manila envelope should be used when mailing your promotional materials. A large envelope is preferred because the resume and cover letter will not have folded lines on them, and they are in perfect condition when opened and first read. The address on the front of the envelope needs to be typewritten either directly on the envelope or on a label. The font should be a legible font such as 12-point Times.

### Fax

Use the same resume for faxing that you would send in the mail. You will want to follow-up your fax by mailing a hard copy of your promotional materials. The fax should only be used when time is of the essence and you need the company to receive the materials immediately. Remember that you lose control over how it comes out on the fax machine and the quality of paper will not be a resume type paper. Therefore, your first impression will not be professional in nature.

## E-mail

If you are sending your resume and cover letter via e-mail, you will want to send them as attachments using a PDF file from your computer (not a scan). This way you have greater control over how your promotional materials appear when the employer first sees them and when your materials are printed. A PDF file is invulnerable to viruses and the document comes across the same as it appears on your computer. However, keep in mind that even though your promotional materials will be formatted correctly, they will still be printed on the wrong type of paper. Remember that you only have one chance to make a first impression.

## Upload to a Website

Many colleges and universities require you to upload your resume and cover letter to their website where a software program will extract keywords from your resume in an attempt to match your qualifications to their job description. This software is known as an applicant tracking system (ATS).

An applicant tracking system is a software system that extracts the information from your resume (known as parsing) and provides hiring managers with information such as your name, address, email address, degrees you've earned, skills you have, and your work experiences.

ATS systems aren't perfect. Depending upon how you format your resume, the system may jumble your information. ATS systems primarily read text; while any extra creativity such as extra spaces, images, large headings, banners, etc. will just present a jumbled mess.

So how do you apply for a job that has you apply online, through an uploaded system? Miguel Forte, from Workable, presents several suggestions for submitting an application via an ATS system including[21]:

- Submit your CV (resume) in a text format preferably .doc or .docx. There are plenty of open source word processors that understand this format these days

- If you use the PDF format, make sure you export it from your word processor – don't scan your CV into an image.

- Try to avoid using headers and footers as they often get interspersed with the main body of text

- Use one standard font throughout the CV

- Don't use tables and columns as the ordering of sentences may not be what you expect

- Don't use WordArt

- Don't fiddle with character spacing

- Write your document on your own computer so that your metadata is correctly set. Text can be found in there too.

- Put your name in the filename of your CV

So, when uploading your resume and cover letter to a college or university's website, make sure you utilize keywords in your resume that correspond with the job description. Also, keep your resume clean and concise, and if you're submitting your information using a PDF, make sure the PDF is sent from a document on your computer and not from a scan (a scan creates a single picture of your information and the computer has a difficult time reading your information).

## Mail versus E-mail

First impressions are huge and this is the reason mailing a resume is preferred over e-mail. When you mail a resume, you have the most control over its appearance – the information appearing formatted correctly, and the use of color, bolding, and underlining. Many employers want you to e-mail, fax, or submit your information to their website. By faxing a document, the date and name of the institution quite often shows up on the top of the page and the transmittal quality is not always great. Therefore, e-mailing your documents using a PDF attachment is preferred to faxing.  But when uploading your resume to a potential employer's website, you are best using a Word Doc for submission of your cover letter and resume.

## Action Steps

Chapter Seven is the first of two chapters that is designed to help you prepare for your job search.  This chapter focused on the development of your promotional materials (your resume, cover letter, and references), and on the development of your personal sales pitch.

**Action Step** – Develop your promotional materials and place them in Section Four of your Workbook Binder.  Your promotional materials include:

  a)   Your Resume

  b)   Your Sample Cover Letter

  c)   Your References

**Action Step** – Complete all three sections of your *Personal Sales Pitch* (Form 5.1) and place it in Section Five in your Workbook Binder.

## CHAPTER 7

# Interview Questions and Final Preparations

The seventh chapter is a continuation from the previous chapter and focuses on preparing you for your job search by having you establish an *Interview Preparation Form*. This form is designed to give you the communicative preparation necessary to be successful during your interview. Also known as an "Interview Cheat Sheet", the *Interview Preparation Form* has five broad areas of preparation:

1. The answers to questions that you are likely to be asked during the interview

2. Your *Personal Sales Pitch* (See Chapter Six)

3. Stories to tell during your interview

4. Questions to ask

5. Closing of the interview

## Interview Preparation Form

The *Interview Preparation Form* is an organized script for you to use during your interview. The first section of this form is an overview of the questions that you might be asked in the interview and your corresponding answers. This is followed by your personal sales pitch. The third and fourth sections outline the stories that you will share with the search committee, followed by questions that you will want to ask during the interview. The final section of the preparation form is an outline of how you will want to close the interview. You will want to keep the *Interview Preparation Form* with you during your interviews so that you can refer to it when necessary. You will also want to use your cheat sheet during telephone interviews and during group interviews. The *Interview Preparation Form* is designed to help guide you through your interview.

Once you have completed writing your *Interview Preparation Form*, you will want to rehearse these answers and stories to memory so they flow easily during an interview. Some people will actually lay the preparation form in front of them and take notes on the cheat sheet during a group interview. In fact, when interviewing over the telephone, your cheat sheet should be organized in a manner that you can glance down and remind yourself of the answer to a particular question. It is best not to actually read from your interview preparation form, rather just refer to it as necessary so that your answers come across fluid and confident in nature.

On the following page is a sample of an *Interview Preparation Form*. It begins with sample questions that you might be asked during an interview, and your corresponding answers. It continues with your sales pitch, stories to tell, questions to ask, and the closing of the interview. The chapter continues by breaking down each of these five sections and explaining how to effectively develop each section. Once each section is explained, you should begin to develop your own *Cheat Sheet*. The final part of the chapter will provide more detail on potential interview questions and suggestions for effectively answering these questions.

# Sample Interview Preparation Form

The following example of an *Interview Preparation Form* is designed to provide you with a method of organizing your interviewing thoughts, answers, questions, and stories. Within each of these sections, only a few examples will be given. Your completed Cheat Sheet will be longer and much more thorough. In fact, the average *Interview Preparation Form* is typically four pages in length.

## Interview Preparation Form

### Section One – Answers to Questions

**Q. What is your philosophy for the athletic department?**

A. We must strive for excellence, while maintaining the utmost integrity. We are in the business of educating young people. As such we want to win championships and graduate our student-athletes.

**Q. What is it about our institution that interests you?**

A. *(Institution)* interests me because it's a *(Division I Institution)*, that is located in *(the State of Iowa)*, and we have many friends and family in and around the *(Des Moines)* area.

*(Tailor each of your three points to the institution where you are interviewing. These points can be its location, the family and friends you have in the area, the type of institution – such as a small private, etc.)*

**Q. What are your strengths and weaknesses?**

A. My strengths are:
   1. I am sincere and genuine
   2. I am respectful of others
   3. I am a positive and optimistic person
   4. I am hardworking and achievement oriented
   5. I am strong with finances

My greatest <u>weakness</u> is:

My <u>networking</u> within college athletics is average. In the past month, I have really worked hard at increasing my knowledge and emphasis on networking.

**Q. Why Should We Hire You?**

A. Use your Sales Pitch

*(Continue by listing all of the anticipated questions: typically, 10-15 questions)*

## Section Two – Personal Sales Pitch

*(Write-in the Sales Pitch that you developed in Chapter Six)*

### Info to convey

I have been in college athletics for over 20 years. My most recent experience was as athletic director at XYZ University. I inherited an XYZ program that lacked success and support.

During my five years as athletic director, we turned the program around and had the most successful sports season in the history of XYZ athletics. In addition, we were 4th in the nation in graduation rates, we significantly increased our fund raising, balanced our budget, and established a reserve account.

### Skills

I am a hard worker who is honest, achievement oriented, respectful of others, good with finances, and I strive to create a department that works together and has a positive work environment.

### Current situation

Currently I am looking to get back into college athletics at an institution that values my experiences, hard work, and integrity.

## Section Three – 5 Success Stories

**Story #1 – Increased the success of the department**
-Strategic Plan (sample)
-Balanced Budget
-Increased Fund Raising
-Made good hires
-4th in nation in graduation rates

**Story #2 – Built new or upgraded facilities for 13 of our 15 sport teams**
-XC Course
-Basketball/Volleyball gym
-Soccer Field
-Football turf

*(Continue with 5 Stories)*

## Section Four - Questions to Ask

1. What are the major issues/challenges facing the athletics department? The institution?

2. What are you looking for in an athletic director?

3. Is the department's budget balanced?

*(Continue with necessary questions: Typically 5-8 questions. Also, use the space provided between questions to write the answer they provided, this information will be used later in the process).*

## Section Five - Closing

1. I appreciate you taking the time to visit with me today.

2. I would like to reiterate that I believe I would be a good fit for this position because I'm (List your 5 skills and traits)
   - Hardworking and achievement oriented
   - Honest and respectful of others
   - Positive, upbeat person
   - Supportive of staff
   - Strong with finances

3. I am interested in the position.

4. Is there anything else I can answer for you or provide for you?

5. What is the next step in the process?

6. Again, thank you for your time.

Form 6.1

## Analyzing Each Section

The following sections provide an analysis of the *Interview Preparation Form* that is presented above. The *Interview Preparation Form* is designed to help you to become prepared for your interview. It is vitally important that once your form is complete, that you practice reciting each section so that you can properly communicate the information in a fluent manner.

### Section 1: Answers to Questions

In this section, you will list the questions that you believe you might be asked during an interview and then provide your corresponding answers. You must then practice answering these questions prior to you having any interviews. You will probably list 10-15 questions and answers. Many of your answers will come from your *Personal Sales Pitch*.

Q. *Potential Interview Question:* What is your Management Style?

A. *Possible Answer to the Question:* As a leader, I have high expectations for our organization and its people. I want to establish a positive climate that is built on hard work, trust, and integrity. I care about the staff both professionally and personally. I believe in hiring good people and empowering them. I believe in having good communication and letting the staff know what is expected of them. I will be there to support the staff but I am definitely not a micro-manager.

Q. *Potential Interview Question:* What can you bring to our company/institution?

A. *Possible Answer to the Question:* I bring to <u>ABC</u> College over 20 years of experience that includes successful positions in <u>marketing</u>, and <u>fund raising</u> (tailor to the position) at the University of _____. I also have an expertise in marketing, and I strive to create a fun and caring environment.

Q. *Potential Interview Question:* What are your strengths and weaknesses?

A. *Possible Answer to the Question:* My <u>strengths</u> are (use your five skills and traits):
  1. I am sincere and genuine
  2. I am respectful of others
  3. I am a positive and optimistic person
  4. I am hardworking and achievement oriented
  5. I am strong with finances

My greatest <u>weakness</u> is:

My <u>networking</u> within college athletics is average. In the past month, I've really worked hard at increasing my knowledge and emphasis on networking.

Q. *Potential Interview Question:* Why Should We Hire You?

A. *Possible Answer to the Question:* Use your Personal Sales Pitch

## Section 2:  Personal Sales Pitch

In chapter six you developed your *Personal Sales Pitch*.  It is the foundation for selling yourself in letters and in interviews.  Your *Personal Sales Pitch* should include three sections – a summary of your resume; your skills, abilities and traits; and your current situation.  Depending upon the question you are asked, you can use the pitch in its entirety or just one of the three sections.  The pitch needs to be geared towards the type of company you are visiting with, whom you are interviewing with, and the position you are seeking.  You will want to communicate your sales pitch clearly and with enthusiasm.  It is important that the interviewing committee understands who you are, what your accomplishments are, and that you are a good fit for the position.

In developing your *Personal Sales Pitch*, the summary of the resume should be a brief overview of your experiences and education, and any accomplishments you might have achieved. In completing the next part of the pitch, (skills, abilities and traits), refer back to your *Assessment Summary* Sheet in chapter four.  It outlines your top skills, traits, and abilities.  The final part of your *Personal Sales Pitch* is a brief summary of what you are currently doing.  You should explain your current position and your short-term career goals and address why you are interviewing.

## Section 3:  5 Success Stories

People like to hear stories.  This section of the *Interview Preparation Form* gets you prepared to answer questions or to give examples of your experience through the use of stories.

In her article, *Ace Behavioral Interviews By Telling Powerful Stories*, Arlene Hirsch discusses how to tell a story.[21]  She writes that a good method for telling stories is based on the PAR format – Problem (or situation), Action, and Result.  A person will want to start their story by describing the problem or situation that they faced.  Next, you need to describe the action that you took.

Finally, you will want to conclude the story by describing the results.

In the article, Hirsch writes that too many people jump right into the actions that they took without completely detailing the problem or situation. She suggests that people need to spend as much time describing the problem as they do in telling the actions that they took. Also, many people get so wrapped up in describing their actions that they forget to adequately describe the results.

In telling a story, be sure to utilize all three parts – describe the problem, communicate the actions that you took, and share the results. Since this is a job interview, make sure that the stories that you tell have a positive message, and that you communicate your stories with energy, enthusiasm and confidence. On the *Interview Preparation Form*, list the title of the story, and then underneath the title, list the main aspects of the story with bullet points. These points might include describing the problem, the actions you took, or the results that were achieved. The purpose of the bullet points is to help you remember the main pieces of the story, so a quick glance at your Cheat Sheet can keep you on track with your story.

## Section 4: Questions to Ask

When preparing for your interview you will want to have the mindset that you are a consultant who is analyzing the organization. Consultants ask questions in an attempt to analyze an organization and to uncover any issues they might face. With this mindset, you need to be prepared to ask direct questions that will help you to understand the organization and their needs. This information is vital in that it will be used later in the interview process and during the follow-up stage in an attempt to influence the people who are making the hiring decisions.

What type of questions would a consultant ask? The first step in this process is to research the company, the position, and the industry. The following are suggestions to help you develop questions. Review the following items and ask the questions who, what, where, why, and when. You should be able to develop some sound questions that will show the company's strengths, weaknesses, and needs.

- Review the organizational structure.
- Who would you report to? Who would report to you?
- What are the duties of the position?
- What are the basic facts about the department?
- Review the mission statement of the university and the athletic or recreation department.
- Review their website.
- Search the Internet for news and information about the university and the department.
- Know the department's competitors.
- Know the demographics of the college.
- Ask colleagues about the university.
- Know who is on the search committee and their backgrounds – It is impressive when you can introduce yourself to them, using their name, before they introduce themselves.
- Ask the search committee what are the greatest challenges facing the university and the athletic department (or recreation department).

## Section 5: Closing – Your Final Sales Job

The closing section of the Interview Preparation Form is an organized method for concluding the interview. It allows you to communicate, and leave a lasting impression to the interview team, as to what your strengths and abilities are, and it lets the members of the search committee know that you are interested in the position. It also provides you with vital information that you can use to your advantage. As you begin to close the interview, you will want to ask non-threatening questions such as – Is there anything else that I can provide for you? What is the next step in the process? The answers to these questions can provide you with information such as how many more applicants will be interviewed, what is their timeline, and it opens the door to provide additional information. The following six steps should be used in properly closing the interview.

1. Let them know that you appreciate them visiting with you

2. Reiterate your five skills and traits from your *Assessment Summary Sheet* in chapter four

3. Let them know that you are interested in the position

4. Ask them if there is anything else you can answer for them or provide for them

5. Find out what the next steps are in the search process

6. Thank the committee for their time


This communication might sound something like this:

*"I appreciate you taking the time to visit with me today. I would like to reiterate that I believe that I would be successful (or a good fit) in this position because I am (list your 5 traits)".*

*"I also want you to know that I am very interested in this position. Is there anything else I can provide for you?"*

*"What is the next step in the process? Again, thank you for taking time to visit with me.*

The closing is the last major sales job for the interview. Do not, however, let your guard down. You are still "on" until you leave campus or no longer have contact with the search committee (possibly at the airport). This, however, is not your last sales job in the process. It is just the last sales job for this interview. Your final sales job will come during the follow-up stage. This will be covered in greater detail in Chapter 10. The next section in this chapter will help you to develop the questions (and answers) that you might be asked during an interview.

## Interview Questions

During the interview, you are being judged on your answers to interview questions, the delivery of your answers, and how you present yourself. Being prepared for these interview questions is essential for a successful interview.

The following lists of questions should give you a good idea of the types of questions that you might be asked. It is important to be prepared for these or similar questions that you believe will be asked during your interview and to articulate your responses effectively. By completing your *Personal Sales Pitch,* you can answer many of these questions by using a part of the pitch or the entire pitch. Many of these questions are open-ended and will allow you to integrate your background, skills, and accomplishments into your answer. Open-ended questions will allow you to present specific examples and include an appropriate story. Remember that preparation is the key to reducing the anxiety that is often associated with interviewing.

## Five Basic Types of Interview Questions

There are five basic types of interview questions. These include personal questions, competency-based questions, performance-based questions, company-based questions, and position-specific questions. For each of these five types of questions, you will want to create a list of questions that might be asked during an interview. You will also want to develop the answers to each of these corresponding questions. List each of these questions and their corresponding answers in a Word document and place it in section one of your *Interview Preparation Form* and also in section seven of your Workbook Binder.

Each of these five types of interview questions will be discussed in greater detail in the sections that follow. These sections will provide sample questions, insight into the purpose of the questions, and how to properly answer each question. This will help you to be prepared to answer the interview questions that you will be asked.

## Personal Questions

Personal questions are questions about you personally. With this type of question, the interviewer may be looking for information on your background, your character, or your value system. Will you be able to represent their organization? Will you get along with the people in the company? The following are examples of personal type questions.

Q. Walk me through your resume?

A. Start with your education and work forward, outlining your employment history and your key accomplishments. Use the resume portion of your pitch.

Q. Tell me about yourself

A. Depending upon when this question is asked, you will need to vary your approach. If this is the first question of the interview, you could use the "walk me through your resume" method. If you have already done this, focus on and state your five strengths.

Q. Where would you like to be in five years?

A. This is asked to see how long you plan to stay in this position or with the organization.

Q. What are your hobbies?

A. They want to see if you would fit in the company.

Q. Why did you leave your last job?

A. Never criticize your past employer or the people in the department. The best answer may be "I left to further my career (education, skills, etc.)"

## Other Personal Questions:

- What two or three accomplishments have given you the most satisfaction?
- What do you do for fun?
- What are your long-term goals?
- What other opportunities/jobs are you looking at?
- Why do you want to relocate to this part of the country?
- How would you describe your leadership style?
- What are your long-term career goals?
- What were the two most important decisions in your life?
- What accomplishment are you most proud of? (One of your stories)
- Why do you want to leave your current position?

## Competency-Based Questions

Competency-Based Questions are designed to find out if you are qualified for the position. What have you accomplished in the past that will show that you will be successful in the future?

Q. Given your background in _____ career, why do you want to be in _____ industry or job? How do you know you will be good at it?

A. Do not be defensive. This is a valid question for someone who is changing careers. In answering this, stress your transferable skills (chapter four), provide an example of when you used the skill, and relate it to the position in which you are interviewing.

Q. What are your strengths?

A. Answer using your *Personal Sales Pitch.*

Q. What are your weaknesses?

A. Be prepared for this question. In most interviews, you will be asked this question. Select a "weakness" that is either benign for the position, or could be interpreted as a strength. (For example, a person with a financial background may say they are detailed oriented, but now they are aware of this tendency and vary their level of detail to accommodate the needs of the project). Never give two weaknesses. Some employers like to sit silently after you provide the answer, hoping that you will begin to feel nervous and that you will continue to talk. Resist this temptation. If the silence is too long and uncomfortable, ask the question – "Did this answer your question?".

## Other Competency-Based Questions:

- How are your communication skills?
- What is your most significant accomplishment in your current position?
- What are your qualifications?
- How would your boss describe you?
- What has been your greatest success? Failure?
- Tell me about a time in your life when you have made a difference. (One of your stories)
- Give an example of a problem you faced and how you solved it.
- What skills will you bring to this position?

## Performance-Based Questions

Performance-based questions can also be classified as behavior-based questions. When answering performance-based questions, you need to be complete and concise with your answer. You first need to understand what is being asked, and then answer it by using the PAR method – describe the <u>problem</u> or situation, what <u>action</u> you took or behavior you used, followed by the <u>result</u> or the outcome of the situation. In essence, you are telling a story about a situation, your action, and the ultimate result.

Q: Tell me about a time when you had to work in a team with a difficult team member?

Q: Give me an example of a difficult problem you've had to deal with and how you gathered information and evaluated it. What was the outcome?

Q. Why should I hire you? (They are looking for the "right fit"). Use your pitch.

## Other Performance-Based Questions:

- What would you like to accomplish in the first 90 days on the job?
- What is your greatest accomplishment?
- As a fundraiser what is the largest gift that you have secured?

## Company-Based Questions

With company-based questions, the search committee wants to see if you are a good fit in their company.

Q. Why do you want to work for us?

A. Approach this from the perspective of what is in it for them, (i.e., because you could make a contribution, you can solve a particular problem they have, etc.).

## Other Company-Based Questions:

- Why our university?
- What makes you want to be a _____ (position you are interviewing for)?

- What makes you think you will be successful as a Director of Recreation?

- In what way do you think you can make a contribution to our company?

- What distinguishes you from the other people we are interviewing today?

## Position-Specific Questions

Position-specific questions are designed to test your knowledge about the actual job. Someone interviewing for a managerial position might be asked questions that relate to his/her management style, their ability to manage budgets, or their experience with a specific position. The best way to generate position-specific questions is to analyze the job announcement and see what duties are required for the position. Then you can take each duty and develop a question, and a corresponding answer to the question, based upon your experience in that area. If you do not have experience in one of the duties, you should study and review the area so that you can intelligently answer questions that pertain to that duty.

Q. What is your management style?

A. If you are interviewing for a management position, anticipate this question and prepare for it. (They want to see if you would be a good fit in their organization)

Q. As a Marketer, have you ever put together a comprehensive marketing plan?

A. (Be prepared and bring a copy of the plan with you to the interview)

Q. As an SID, do you have some examples of the media guides that you have designed and the press releases you have written?

A. (Anticipate this and bring samples to the interview)

Q. What are the most important issues facing Division II athletics?

A. If you are interviewing for an athletic director's position at a Division II institution, you will most likely be asked this question (They want to see if you are in tune with the industry).

## Other Position-Specific Questions:

- What is your leadership style?
- How would you set-up a fund raising campaign?
- How would you write a press release?
- What is a zero-based budget?
- Who would you hire as your assistant coaches?

# Top 10 Interviewing Questions

Below are the most frequent interview questions that are asked in an interview.

1. "Walk me through your resume" or "Tell me about yourself".

2. What are your strengths? Weaknesses?

3. What is your management style?

4. Why do you want to leave your current position?

5. What is it about our institution that interests you? (Why do you want to work for our institution?)

6. What can you bring to our institution?

7. What is the purpose of athletics on a college campus?

8. What are your career goals?

9.  What would your last supervisor say about you?

10. Why should we hire you?

## Preparing Your Stories

This section is designed to help you be organized for when you tell your stories. People like to hear stories and examples. Think of some experiences or examples of the more successful events in your life. It might be helpful to refer back to chapter four and the *Motivated Strengths and Enjoyable Activities Exercise* that you completed. In organizing the story, begin by writing out the title of the event. Next, write a word or short phrase to describe the problem, and continue by describing the action that you took and the results that occurred. These descriptions will become bullet points that will be used in the third section of the *Interview Preparation Form.* Be prepared to use one or more of these stories during your interview session.

### Stories Worksheet

**Directions:** List the name of the event or the story that you are describing. Next, list a word or short phrase that will help you to remember the problem, action, and result of each story. Upon completion of this worksheet, include an outline of your stories on the third section of your *Interview Preparation Form.*

Story Title #1_____

Summarize/Outline of major points

Problem:_____

Action: _____

Result: _____

Story Title #2_____

Summarize/Outline of major points

Problem:_____

Action: _____

Result: _____

*Continue with this format until you have four or more stories completed.*

Form 6.2

# How to Answer Interview Questions

When answering an interview question, you first need to understand what is being asked and then keep your answer brief. If you begin to stray from the question or you begin to ramble, return to your sales pitch and discuss your traits or skills and show the search committee how you can solve their problems. Once you finish your answer, feel free to wrap up your answer with a question such as "does this answer your question?". Your answer should never be longer than two minutes.

While answering the interview questions, you will want to make sure that you are positive in all of your interactions. Do not let your guard down and say something negative about a former boss. By being negative you will most likely turn off the interviewers and lose the job. People want to be around upbeat, positive people and therefore you need to answer your questions in a positive manner. Always remember not to let your guard down, even during breaks in the interview.

As you prepare for the interview, if your resume or background presents a red flag, such as a gap in your employment history, you will need to be prepared to address this so that you come across in a confident and poised manner. Keep eye contact with the people who are interviewing you. In a group setting, make sure to look at each person without solely focusing on only one or two people. Always be truthful as you answer a question, go ahead and put a positive spin on it but be truthful. Finally, as the interview unfolds and you are becoming more comfortable with the members of the search committee, do not let your guard down. Quite often, when people feel comfortable with one another, they tend to relax and "open up". Resist this temptation because what you say will last with the members of the committee. Instead, be like a politician. If a tough question is asked, a politician will often answer a question indirectly by presenting the information they want you to understand – i.e. revert back to your sales pitch and show how you can help to solve their problems. Do not forget to tie a story or two into your answers. People like to hear stories.

## Answering Illegal Questions

There are certain questions that are illegal to ask in an interview. Federal and State law does not allow a person to be discriminated upon in the hiring process. The United States Equal Employment Opportunities Commission (EEOC) has outlined six areas in which it is illegal to discriminate when making employment decisions.[22] These include:

- Sex
- Race
- Age
- Religion
- Ethnic Group
- Disability

Even though it is illegal to ask questions regarding these subjects, quite often during interviews an illegal question is asked. How do you answer these questions? For example, an illegal question might be asked in a social setting with no ill intent. The person might ask you "So, what year did you graduate from high school?" The socially graceful thing to do might be to just answer the question. But what if the person asking the question is really wondering how old you are and if you have the energy to work overtime or travel out of town?

At this point you have three choices: (a) to answer the question, (b) to answer what you believe they are trying to ask, or (c) to not answer the question. If you choose not to answer the question, you could attempt to gracefully change the subject. This might be a little awkward, but it can be effective if it is done gracefully. If you answer the question based on what you believe the intent of the question is, it could sound something like this "If you are wondering if I am available to work overtime and travel out of town, yes I am." Regardless of how you choose to answer these questions, it can be a bit uncomfortable. However, if you choose to answer the question, you will probably want to keep your response short and succinct, and move on to the next topic.

## Questions Not to Ask

Be aware of the types of questions you should not ask during an interview. The goal is to build positive relationships during your meetings and to show that you have done your research. Avoid the possibility of making the interviewer feel uncomfortable or to show that you have not adequately prepared for the interview.

- Avoid asking questions that are answered in the institution's general information or on their website (e.g. number of sports offered, the record of last year's team, etc.). These types of questions will let the interviewer know that you did not do your homework. But by all means ask questions if some information is not clear to you.

- Avoid asking about the salary or benefits in the first interview. This is a major mistake. Quite often, the salary can be found on the Internet or in a published article. The interviewer may choose to bring up this information, but you should not initiate the topic. By asking about the salary too early in the process, you will give the impression that you are more concerned with what is in it for you. In fact, the interviewer may give you the salary range up front to see if you are still interested. If the salary is a bit low, do not say it is. Allow the process to take its course. If you are their choice, you can attempt to negotiate a better salary. However, do not think that you can get the hiring manager to increase the salary by 25-50 percent. This is a waste of time for both you and the hiring institution.

- Avoid asking any personal questions or questions that will put the recruiter on the defensive. These may include, but are not limited to: their age, race, religion, health, or marital status.

- Avoid asking questions that have already been answered in the interview session that you are currently in. If some of the questions on your list have already been answered during the current session, do not repeat them. However, feel free to ask the same question to different people, especially if you are not comfortable with the answer you received.

## Action Steps

**Action Step** – Create an *Interview Preparation Form* (Form 6.1) and add it to Section Six in your binder. You will need to practice answering the questions, using your sales pitch, telling your stories, asking questions, and closing the interview. You might want to practice alone, with a friend, or by talking into a tape recorder. Regardless of your personal style, you need to practice, and practice a lot.

**Action Step** – Complete your *Stories Worksheet* (Form 6.2) and place it in Section Six in your Worksheet Binder. Also include your stories worksheet in the third section of your *Interview Preparation Form.*

**Action Step** – Develop a list of questions that you might be asked during an interview. Create an answer for each of the corresponding questions. Add these interview questions and your answers (Form 7.1) to Section Seven of your Worksheet Binder. Also, include your list of interview questions and the corresponding answers to the first section of your *Interview Preparation Form*.

# CHAPTER 8

---

# Promoting Yourself

A promotional campaign is a focused approach designed to make customers aware of a particular product, brand, or service.[23] The campaign has a set of objectives and uses a variety of strategies and techniques to promote the product.[24] In your job search campaign both the product and the brand are you, and the objective is to promote you to the organizations within your target market.

There are five stages that are included within a promotional campaign.[25] These include:

1. The objective(s) of the promotional campaign
2. The identification of the target market
3. Which promotional techniques to use
4. Which promotional materials to use
5. How the campaign should be monitored and evaluated

From the previous chapters, you have already developed three of the five steps of your promotional campaign. You have established the objective(s) for your campaign – to promote yourself to the organizations within your target market. You have also identified the organizations that are in your target market. Finally, you have created your promotional materials – your resume, your *Personal Sales Pitch*, the cover letter, and your list of references.

In addition to developing these three steps, you have also prepared yourself to be able to answer interview questions, to ask questions, and to tell stories through developing your *Interview Preparation Form*. Therefore, you are now ready for the fourth step, to develop the promotional strategies and techniques that will be used in your job search campaign. The fifth and final step in the job search process will be for you to monitor and evaluate your campaign. Therefore, the focus of this chapter is to provide you with strategies and techniques that you can use to promote yourself to the colleges within your target market, and then to monitor and evaluate the process.

# Promoting Yourself

One of the most important aspects of an effective job search campaign is for a person to properly promote themselves to the institutions that are within their target market. Promoting yourself is letting people know about you, about your skills and competencies, and about your interests. There are two basic ways in which people promote themselves – through developing their brand image, and through making connections.

## Creating Your Brand Image

According to the American Marketing Association, a brand is a name or feature that distinguishes one seller's product from another seller's product.[26] This feature can be a product name such as "Diet Coke", a slogan such as "Just Do It", a color such as powder blue being associated with the UNC Tar Heels, or an image that is associated with a product such as Notre Dame football.

According to researchers, a brand produces "sensations, feelings, cognitions, and behavioral responses evoked by brand-related stimuli. These brand-related stimuli are generated "as part of a brand's design and identity, packaging, communication, and environments."[27] In other words, we think, have emotions toward, and ultimately respond to a product's brand. This brand is determined by its image, how it is packaged, and how it is sold to us. People also have brands. What images are formed when sports figures such as Lance Armstrong, Dennis Rodman, Tiger Woods, or Michael Jordan are mentioned? All four conjure up different images, and these images are how they are perceived. This perception is their brand image.

The American Marketing Association defines a brand image as the perception that people have of a particular product.[28] This perception of a person is not always accurate, but it is the perception that has been developed through their image, skills, actions, and professionalism.

Montoya, in his book *The Brand Called You*, states that the most important element of a successful personal brand is a person's specialization. In other words, what are you known for? Montoya suggests that a person should develop a specialization statement. This statement would state three things: (a) who you are, (b) what you do, and (c) for whom you do it.[29]

So, what is your brand? What image do people have of you? What do you want your brand to be? In order to develop a strong brand, you need to identify what you want to be known for. In other words, what is your specialization? Some coaches want to be known as a great recruiter, and others want to be known as an expert in teaching their sport. Certain sports administrators are experts in marketing or fund raising, while others are experts in compliance. You will want to begin to identify your area of specialization by developing your *Personal Branding Statement*. This statement should identify (a) the industry in which you want to be known for your expertise (e.g. intercollegiate sports, recreational sports, etc.). (b) your profession (e.g. sports information, marketing, soccer coaching), (c) your area of specialization (e.g. game operations, licensing, recruiting the NWAACC), and (d) your target market.

In developing your *Personal Branding Statement* (and thus your area of expertise), you will want to identify and select a very narrow segment of the profession in which you will specialize. If your area is too broad, you will become a generalist and not a specialist. It is this act of specializing that helps to brand you as an expert within the profession.

For example, if you are a coach and you want to become known as a great recruiter, you might want to specialize in recruiting student-athletes from a certain segment of the population. Maybe you specialize in recruiting players from community colleges. To further narrow your focus, you might want to specialize in recruiting student-athletes from the NWAACC conference (community colleges in Washington and Oregon).

As you begin to develop your plan for becoming the best recruiter of student-athletes who participate in the NWAACC, you will want to include in your plan the goal of getting to know all of the head coaches whose teams participate in your sport and are members of the NWAACC. You will also want to attend their contests, championships, and to become an extended part of their coaching group. This same level of specialization can be developed in administration.

As an athletic administrator, you will want to specialize in a profession within intercollegiate athletics such as sports marketing. You will then want to further narrow your area of specialization to a segment of marketing such as product licensing. You would still need to fully understand sports marketing, but you would become an expert in the area of collegiate licensing.

As you begin to focus on licensing, you will want to study everything you can about it and become active in the national association that serves collegiate licensing (International

Collegiate Licensing Association). You will also need to become familiar with how athletic departments generate money from selling licensed products, and know who are the major licensing companies. In addition, you will want to network with other professionals who specialize in licensing. This type of segmenting within an industry can be used in nearly every aspect of coaching or sports administration, and can help you to identify an area in which you can eventually become an expert. This type of specialization does not mean that you ignore the rest of the profession, it just means that within your marketing duties, you are an expert in this one segment of the profession – licensing.

So how do you get started in specializing? How do you become an expert? Keith Ferrazzi, from Inc.com found his niche by having an interest in a particular area. He then "studied all texts that were available, interviewed experts at conferences, and endlessly discussed and debated the issues with my colleagues." He then started to write articles on the subject of his expertise, he taught the subject within the company where he was employed, and he then began to speak about the subject at conferences. Ferrazzi believes that becoming an expert is a simple formula – first you need to build your expertise, and then you need to get people to recognize you as an expert.[30]

To further enhance your brand, you will want to join your professional association, attend conferences and workshops, and meet other colleagues within your profession. Find out from your readings and conversations what the hot topics are within the profession. Try to find a subject that is not being adequately addressed and write a research article about the topic. Identify which journals or publications would publish articles within your profession, and submit an article for publication. Expand your exposure through public speaking. If you are uncomfortable with public speaking, take a speech class or join an organization such as Toastmasters.

In addition to specializing in a particular segment of the sports profession, your brand will be shaped by your image. Your image is a reflection of your activities, actions, and behaviors. In other words, a person's image is shaped by how they live their life, the products they buy, the way they dress, and how professional they are in what they say and do. Therefore, your image can be shaped by the type of car you drive, the type of clothes you wear, how you conduct yourself in a social setting, and through the type of language you use. A person might be perceived as being disciplined, being a professional, being a hard worker, or being very knowledgeable about their profession. Still others might be perceived as not being very good at what they do, or being unprofessional. Make sure that your actions and behaviors align with the brand that you want for yourself.

Developing your brand image is a marathon and not a sprint. You cannot wake up one morning and declare that you are an expert on something, and then subsequently be recognized as an expert. However, you can begin slowly by studying all that you can about a certain topic, by joining the association for your profession, and by meeting other professionals. The main concept is that you need to prove yourself within the profession by working hard to become an expert in your field, and to gain the respect of your colleagues.

## Developing Connections

The second way to promote yourself is through establishing and enhancing relationships with people. People typically get jobs through having a connection within the organization. According to Kris Plantrich of ResumeWonders Writing and Career Coaching Services, "65-70% of jobs are gained through personal referrals or networking connections."[31] Therefore, whether it is through directly knowing the hiring manager or knowing someone who knows the people on the search committee, it is important for you to have a connection with the people who are doing the hiring.

According to the Texas Job Hunter's Guide, "connecting is the process of giving and receiving in all of your relationships" and "it's the best way to find a job."[32] Therefore in order to give yourself the very best opportunity for securing a job, you need to establish and build connections within your profession.

The better you know someone (assuming they trust you and they respect your skills), the more likely it is that they will hire you when they have a job opening. This is why networking is the most effective method for searching for a job. At the other end of the job search spectrum, is blindly answering an advertisement. The likelihood of getting a job through answering an advertisement, when you do not have a connection with the hiring manager, is extremely remote. Chances are that somebody who has a connection with the hiring manager is also applying for the same job. The difference between networking and blindly answering an advertisement is in the strength of your connection with the hiring manager. In networking, the hiring manager knows and trusts you. Whereas, in applying for a position through an advertisement, the hiring manager does not know you and you are just one of several applicants.

An example of this networking connection is seen when a major university hires a coach from a school in a different conference. While the athletic director may or may not personally know the coach with whom they want to hire, the athletic director most likely knows somebody who knows the coach. But it works both ways. Most likely the coach knows somebody who knows the athletic director. In essence, the world of college sports is a relatively small fraternity and everyone knows one-another. This might be a bit of a stretch, but everyone within the industry probably knows somebody who knows the person doing the hiring. Therefore, it is relatively safe to say that there is no more than one person of separation between an applicant who is currently working in college sports, and the person doing the hiring in another athletic department.

While it is true that a good hiring manager will actively recruit for a major position, it is also true that you cannot leave it to chance that an employer will come looking for you when they have a job available. It is much more likely, however, that they will call you when they have a job available if they know you, know that you are good at what you do, and know that you would be a good fit for the institution.

Therefore, you need to actively and effectively promote yourself to others within the profession through such methods as networking and direct contact. As with developing your brand, building and maintaining your contacts is a long-term activity. Begin developing your contacts today, so that you have the proper connections tomorrow when the job you want becomes available.

# Promotional Techniques

As was discussed earlier, there are two basic ways to promote a person – through creating brand awareness and through making connections with the people within the industry. Techniques for developing both of these methods of promoting yourself are outlined and discussed in the sections that follow.

## Techniques for Branding Yourself

In developing your brand identity, there are several techniques that can be used that are effective in establishing a person's brand. One of the first steps in developing a personal brand is to develop your personal branding statement. This is a statement that defines what you do and who you serve. It includes identifying the industry where you work (e.g. intercollegiate athletics), your profession (e.g. sports information), your area of specialization (e.g. game operations), and the target market that you are pursuing (e.g. college athletic departments in Iowa). Other items that you will want to consider when developing your brand identity is to be aware of your image, to join the professional association that serves the area of your specialization, and to begin to write and publish articles within the topic of your expertise.

By focusing on these techniques, you will begin to brand yourself as an expert in your field. These techniques, therefore, should be included in your branding plan, and are described in greater detail below.

**Specialize** – Specializing is the key element to creating your brand. What are you known for? What do you want to be known for? What area of the profession excites you? What area of the profession are you passionate about? If there is a profession within the industry that excites you, choose that as your area in which to specialize. Your first step in creating your personal brand needs to be in identifying an area (profession) within a particular industry, and this area needs to capture your passion, excitement, and enthusiasm. Begin by reading and studying the various topics within the industry. Your goal needs to be to work within an area that interests you, and then to start to specialize in a specific segment within that profession. This would be similar to the example that was previously introduced where a person could work in marketing and specialize in licensing. Once you have identified your area of specialization you will now want to write your personal branding statement.

**Personal Branding Statement** – Once you have established the area in which you want to specialize, you will now develop a branding plan by writing your personal branding statement. Your personal branding statement will identify the industry in which you work (e.g. intercollegiate athletics, recreational sports), your profession (e.g. sports information, marketing, soccer coach), your area of specialization (e.g. game operations, licensing, recruiting the NWAACC), and the target market that you are pursuing (e.g. college athletic departments in Iowa). This branding statement will help guide you as you begin to promote yourself. Refer to the third worksheet within the Job Search Campaign (Form 8.3). It is designed to assist you in identifying the elements that are included in your personal branding statement. Use this worksheet to develop your statement and to create a plan for developing your personal brand.

**Join A Professional Association** – One of the key elements to becoming known in any industry is to get to know the people associated with the profession. With this in mind, your next step in developing your personal brand is to identify and join the associations for your profession (e.g. marketing) and your area of specialization (e.g. licensing). By joining a professional association, you will have an opportunity to learn all that you can about the profession by reading the latest information, to meet other colleagues within the profession, and to be able to stay connected with these colleagues through a common interest – the professional association.

**Be Aware of Your Image** – Your image is the perception that others have of you. It is a reflection of your activities, actions, and behaviors. Make sure that your lifestyle is congruent with the image that you want for your brand. This holds true for both your personal and professional life. At some point your personal and professional life will become intertwined and become one in the same.

**Writing and Publishing** – One of the best ways to become recognized as an industry expert is to write about topics within your area of specialization and to become published. Find a topic within your specialization that interests you. Research that topic and write a research paper about the subject. This could be as simple as interviewing the leading professionals within the profession, or identifying the proper fundamental techniques that are utilized within your area of specialization. Once you have written the paper, submit it for publication to a journal that serves your profession. As you begin to become published, you will start to become recognized as an expert in the profession.

**Public Speaking** – Another way to become recognized as an expert is through public speaking. As you write your papers and submit them for publication, turn them into speeches. Contact the local Kiwanis Clubs and Rotary Clubs and share your expertise with them. Contact your professional association and submit a proposal for a presentation at a regional or national conference.

**Conference/Regional Championships** – Another method for branding yourself is to work at conference championship events and at the NCAA Regional sporting events. You will gain great knowledge in how the most organized and prepared sports contests are conducted. These are also great ways to network within the profession, and you will be associated with the best people in the industry.

## Techniques for Making Connections

Making connections is the process of building relationships with people. Of the various methods for making connections, networking is the best way to build these relationships. In fact, over time, networking is the best way to get a job because you will have a personal relationship with the person doing the hiring. By having a personal relationship with the person doing the hiring, you naturally have an "in" with the company.

There are four basic types of making connections – direct contact, networking, informational interviews, and entry-level positions. These four strategies are discussed in the next sections, but since networking is the best way for a person to get a job, an entire section is devoted to the networking process later in this chapter.

**Direct Contact** – Direct contact is where you personally contact people through face-to-face meetings, telephone conversations, mail, or e-mail. Direct contact can range from applying for a job by responding to an advertisement in a newspaper or website, to participating in networking opportunities at conferences and conventions. Direct contact is the key to building relationships, and having strong relationships is the key to getting a job.

**Networking** – Networking is the establishing of personal relationships with colleagues within your profession. It usually starts out by you meeting a colleague through direct contact, and as time passes, the relationship grows stronger and develops into a professional relationship. Networking is about building relationships. These relationships should be beneficial to both of you; not just a means for getting a job. Even so, networking is the most effective method for getting a job.

There are several ways to meet colleagues and to build a strong network. One of the most effective ways to build a strong network is through attending professional conferences and conventions. Plan to attend the educational seminars and the social gatherings at these events and introduce yourself to other attendees. Have your business cards available and give them to the people you meet. Be discrete when passing out your business cards, do not make it appear as if you are blanketing the social with them. Only pass your cards out to people with whom you have had a quality conversation. Show interest in them, and at the end of the conversation ask them if they have a business card. Exchange cards and move on to your next conversation. Stay in contact with the people you meet and begin to build your network within the profession.

Another method for beginning to build a networking relationship is to identify a mentor, and develop a mentorship. A mentorship is where an experienced professional (mentor) provides guidance and insights to a less experienced person (mentee). The mentee is typically relatively new to the profession and is seeking to learn more about the industry or the profession. The relationship usually begins with an informational interview, where many questions about the profession are asked. From this meeting, a formal or informal mentorship can begin. A formal mentorship is where the interviewee asks the professional if he or she would be their mentor. Whereas, an informal mentorship is where a person builds a relationship with a professional but does not formally ask them to be a mentor. In an informal mentorship, a person can continue to seek guidance and insights without formally asking the professional if he or she would be their mentor.

Networking is the single most effective way to build relationships and ultimately to get a job. The key to networking is to be active in your profession and to build strong relationships that are beneficial to both you and your network.

**Informational Interviews** – One of the most effective ways to begin the networking process and learn more about the profession is through conducting an informational interview. An informational interview is a form of both direct contact and networking. It is an effective way to get to know people within an organization and to get to know more about the company itself. An informational interview is where an entry-level person interviews a coach or athletic administrator in an attempt to find out more about the profession or industry. The interview typically lasts about an hour and is conducted in the office of the coach or administrator.

**Shadowing** – Shadowing is a type of informational interview. It is an extended form of the interview and typically includes following (shadowing) a professional throughout the business day so that you can see what their job entails. This is an effective way for an entry-level person to gain insights into a profession and to begin the networking process.

**Entry-level Positions** – Internships, graduate assistantships, and volunteering your services are forms of both direct contact and networking. However, securing an entry-level position is even more effective than an informational interview is, in building relationships with people within an organization. This is because the people within the institution where you are working will have an opportunity to see how hard you work, the quality of your work, and will begin to build a relationship with you. Therefore, if you are looking to break into the sports industry, include one or more of these types of opportunities in your promotional campaign.

## Networking – The Best Way to Get a Job

By now you know that networking is the most effective way of getting a job. Knowing the person who is doing the hiring gives an applicant an advantage over the other applicants. However, networking is much more than getting to know people so they can help you to get a job. According to the Careers Office at MIT, networking is "a planned process in which you will interact with and become known, through formal and informal settings."[33]

According to The Riley Guide, "networking is the art of building alliances".[34]

These alliances will definitely help you when it comes to applying for a job, but it is much more than this. Strong alliances will also help you in enhancing your knowledge within the profession through the sharing of concepts and ideas. Coaches will get together and X & O with one another. X and O's are diagramming of plays and strategies within a particular sport. Administrators do not tend to spend as much time individually with other administrators; rather they discuss sports business concepts in conference business meetings, regional seminars, and at national conventions. Whether you are Xing & Oing as a coach, or sharing concepts and ideas as an administrator, building contacts and sharing knowledge with colleagues is a vitally important and enjoyable aspect of networking.

While networking and building alliances are similar in most industries, there is a definite difference in how coaches and athletic administrators go about building connections. Because sports teams compete against one another, coaches will meet other coaches during these competitions. Although coaches are fiercely competitive during the contest, they tend to be friendly and supportive of their colleagues once the contest is over. Building a network through competing against one another is unique to coaches, and is not typically a viable networking alternative for an administrator.

Administrators, such as associate and assistant athletic directors, typically do not travel with their sports teams and therefore they do not have access to building relationships with other administrators during sporting events. The exception to this would be in Division I football and men's basketball. In these sports, the athletic director (or a designated representative), along with the sports information director, an athletic trainer, and sometimes the ticket manager, will travel with the team. These administrators, of course, will have a greater opportunity to meet colleagues and other athletic administrators during these events. However, this access to networking during an event is typically limited to Division I football and basketball.

These are just a couple of examples that show the differences in how networking is different for coaches and athletic administrators. Other types of networking techniques for coaches and athletic administrators are discussed in the following sections.

## Networking – Coaching

Networking as a coach is different than networking in most professions. This is due to the nature of the coaching profession. As was mentioned previously, coaches get to know other coaches through competing against one another. This is just one of several ways in which coaches build their network within their profession.

In order to effectively network as a coach in college sports, you need to be active professionally in your sport. This starts by having you work summer camps at major universities, and by attending regional coaching clinics. Working summer camps at major universities is emphasized because other top-level coaches will also be working these camps. The coaches who work the camps at major universities are the future national leaders within your sport. However, do not overlook working the local and regional camps and clinics. Working these camps and clinics will help you to meet and build relationships with the coaches within your region. In essence, you need to build relationships with as many people within your sport as possible.

As you meet other coaches, stay in contact with them. Send them e-mails of support and periodic letters to update them about your team. Attend your national convention, such as the Final Four in men's basketball, and strengthen the relationships with these coaches. Meet the friends of your colleagues and begin to build relationships with these new acquaintances. Continue with this process and continue to build your alliances. In a matter of a few years, you will have established a strong network within your sport.

In time, a person can build a large and strong network of colleagues within the coaching ranks. This is built through being active in your sport, by working camps, attending clinics, and attending the national conventions. In essence you are building life-long friendships through being active in your sport. This is how you network in the coaching ranks because your alliances are your friends, and when you are in need of something (such as a job), they will be there for you. Conversely, when they need something, you will be there for them as well. This is what friends do.

## Networking – Administration

Networking in athletic administration is a different process than it is in coaching. In coaching, you build relationships with other coaches when your teams compete against each other, and you meet coaches at summer camps, and at coaching clinics. While an athletic director or an associate athletic director might travel with the football team or with the men's basketball team, typically administrators do not meet other administrators in the same way as coaches meet other coaches.

So how does a marketing director or a compliance officer meet other athletic administrators from other colleges? Athletic administrators usually meet other athletic administrators while attending conference (or league) meetings, regional seminars, and at national conventions. If you do not attend any of these conferences, then it is difficult to build a network within your profession. For example, if you are the marketing director within an athletic department, you should be attending the National Association of Collegiate Marketing Administrators (NACMA) meeting every June. NACMA provides forums for administrators to share information, and socials to get to know one another. NACMA is affiliated with the athletic director's professional association – NACDA. Each area of specialization within college athletics has a professional association. Many of these associations are affiliated with NACDA.

Once you begin to meet other professionals within your area of interest, you need to cultivate these connections and build alliances. But you also need to find other ways to meet more people within your profession. Through your area of specialization, you can attend workshops and conferences that are specifically designed for your specialization. For example, if you are a business manager in an athletic department, how do you get to know other business managers and how do you get to know athletic directors? Jaime Pollard who is the athletic director at Iowa State University was the Deputy Athletic Director for Business at the University of Wisconsin. He was active in his professional association, the College Athletic Business Management Association (CABMA). Being extremely active in the association, he would eventually serve as the association's president.

In addition to his duties at Wisconsin and his involvement with CABMA, Jaime started a side business, Collegiate Financial Services. With Collegiate Financial Services, Jaime would compile financial information and provide customized financial reports to universities and conference commissioners. He began to present his findings and concepts at the NACDA conventions. This led him to build a large and strong network of friends and colleagues within the world of college athletics, and to be recognized as an expert in the field of finances within Division I college athletic departments.[35] This reputation as an expert in finances within Division I helped Jamie to become a Division I athletic director at Iowa State University.

## Networking – In General

So you can see that networking is much more than just meeting people, it is getting to know them as friends. You need to see the "big picture" and understand that both networking and your career are long-term ventures.

If you are just starting out, visit with others within the profession. Introduce yourself and inquire if you can ask them a few questions. In other words, conduct an informational interview. As you are starting your career, befriend others who are also just starting out. Help each other within the profession and work together in getting to know even more professionals within the industry. Seek out a mentor, such as the athletic director at your school, or an associate athletic director at another school. While these mentors will not be your direct colleagues, they will be an invaluable source for knowledge and direction within the industry. You will also be building a relationship and an alliance with them. However, your strongest relationships will be with your friends and colleagues. These friends and colleagues will slowly move up the ladder within the profession (and so will you), and as time passes, your group will eventually be the leaders within the profession.

This is how networking works. You need to view networking as a long-term process. You need to view the purpose of a networking meeting as an opportunity to build a relationship and gain insight into the industry, not to get a job. Getting a job from the assistance of your contacts will happen, it just takes time.

Therefore, the objective of networking is to try to build long-term relationships with people. You start by arranging an informational meeting at their office where you ask sincere questions that will help you to grow in the profession. Do not think that the informational interview will land you a job. It is an opportunity to gain knowledge and to build a relationship. Make sure that you properly thank the person you met with, and then stay in contact with them.

As you actively work on getting to know more people within the industry and build relationships with them, your network will continue to grow. While you did not set out to get a job from your contacts, as you build your network and you have strong and sincere relationships, your contacts will recommend you for a job when the right job does become available. Make sure that you are patient with the process, you work hard at your current job, and that you stay in contact with the people within your network.

Things worthwhile truly do take time. Remember, it is estimated that 65-70 percent of all jobs are found through personal referrals or networking connections.[36]

## Networking (and Informational Interview) Format

As you prepare for an informational interview, you will want to know what format you will use to interact in the meeting. Be prepared and have a set of questions that you will ask. Bring a copy of your resume and be prepared to share it with them if they ask. Do not provide them with a resume if they do not ask for one. You are not at the meeting trying to get a job, and you do not want the meeting to come off as such. Therefore, the following is a suggested outline to follow.

**Introduction** – Introduce yourself and graciously thank them for seeing you. Some small talk (two to three sentences) might be appropriate to break the ice.

**Tell Them Why You Wanted To See Them** – Be honest and let them know that you wanted to know more about the industry or the profession. Tell them that you know that they are busy and that you will not take too much of their time.

**Tell Them About Yourself** – This is a chance to sell yourself by sharing your story (your Personal Sales Pitch). Keep it relatively short and do not put them to sleep with your life story – just the highlights.

**Ask Questions** – Make sure that you prepare thoroughly for your meeting and have a list of questions that you want to ask. Remember, you are interviewing them. See the sample questions in the next section of this chapter for some ideas. Make sure that you take notes during the meeting.

**Ask For Referrals** – Find out who else you should contact within the industry. As he or she provides you with names, ask them if you can mention their name as the one who recommended that you contact them.

**Thank Them** – Being careful not to abuse their time, graciously thank them for their time and ask them if they would mind if you stayed in touch with them.

**Follow-up** – Send a thank you letter to them and personalize it from the notes from the meeting. Continue to stay in contact with them (even a short note) every three to four months. Provide them with a status report on yourself and the progress you have made within the profession.

## Possible Networking Questions

You need to be prepared with a list of questions that you want to ask during the informational interview. Remember that you are interviewing them so that you can gain insight and knowledge into the profession; they are not interviewing you. Do not even begin to think that they will suggest hiring you. The questions that you ask should be sincere questions that can help you in your quest to be involved in the industry. Possible questions can follow the "who, what, where, why, and how" within the industry. The following questions would be appropriate for an informational interview within intercollegiate athletics.

### The Industry

- Who actually is the NCAA?
- What do you believe is the future of college athletics?
- Where should I go to get my master's degree in Sports Management?
- Why is it important to become a coach if I want to be an athletic director?
- How does a conference or league function?

### Jobs

- Who oversees the finances in a college athletic department?
- What does an SID do?

- Where does a compliance officer turn for answers to questions they might have?
- Why do athletic departments have faculty athletic representatives?
- How does athletic fund raising work?

## Institution

- Who does an athletic director report to?
- What is the structure of the athletic department?
- Where do the student-athletes go if they have academic needs?
- Why do the freshmen student-athletes have to live in the residence halls?
- How is the booster club structured?

## The Person You Are Meeting

- Were you an athlete in college?
- What are your career goals?
- Where did you go to college?
- Why did you pursue fund raising prior to being an athletic director?
- How did you become an athletic director?

The importance of networking as a method of promoting yourself cannot be over-emphasized. While networking is one of the key methods for securing a job, keep in mind that it is just one of various techniques that can be used in making a connection with people within your target market. As you begin to plan your job search campaign, you will want to use several of these various promotional techniques to effectively promote yourself. Plan to promote yourself both through developing your brand image, and through making connections with people within your target market. Both of these methods need to be included in your job search campaign.

In the next section, you will be asked to develop a job search campaign. This campaign will include all five stages that were introduced in the promotional campaign at the beginning of the chapter. Each of these stages will be discussed in detail, and five worksheets are included that will help you to begin to build an organized and focused campaign for your upcoming job search.

## The Job Search Campaign

To effectively search for a job, a person will want to develop an organized job search campaign. This type of campaign will include the five stages of a promotional campaign that were introduced at the beginning of the chapter. These stages are:

1. The objectives of the campaign

2. The identification of your target market

3. The promotional techniques that you will use

4. The promotional materials that you will use

5. The methods that will be utilized to monitor and evaluate the campaign

To begin the process of developing a job search campaign, an overview of the campaign is provided in *The Campaign Overview* (Form 8.1), which is presented later in the chapter. This overview outlines each step that will be used to develop the Job Search Campaign. The overview is the first of five worksheets that will be used in building this comprehensive and focused campaign. The second worksheet (Form 8.2) expands upon the overview and will have you state the objectives of the campaign, list your target market, identify which promotional techniques you will use, identify which promotional materials you will use, and it provides the criteria that you should use to monitor and evaluate the campaign.

The third worksheet, *Creating Your Brand* (Form 8.3), is designed to help assist you with the creation of your brand image. It will have you identify your area of specialization and the elements that you need in order to build an effective brand.

A fourth worksheet (Form 8.4) is designed to help you identify how you will penetrate and connect with each institution within your target market. Upon completion of this form you will begin working on your final worksheet, the *Institutional Summary Sheet* (Form 8.5). The Institutional Summary Sheet has you provide contact information for each organization within your target market, and it has you list all of the interactions that you have had with the people at that organization. You will have a separate Institutional Summary Sheet for each organization that is listed in your target market.

As you develop your job search campaign, and strategize about how you will connect with each institution, most of your connecting will be done in the form of networking. However, you will also be connecting by applying for jobs through classified advertisements in trade journals, newspapers, websites, and through search firms. As you apply for jobs, you will want to see if any of your close colleagues have connections with people who are employed at the organization where you are applying. This can help provide you with referrals for the open position, and having referrals is one of the keys elements to having an "in" with the hiring committee.

Depending upon the stage of your career, techniques that you use within your campaign will differ. For example, people who are just starting out in their professional career may focus on having an informational interview, and maybe volunteering at the local athletic department. Whereas, a person with more experience might decide to focus on networking, writing, publishing in journals, and speaking at conferences and conventions.

Regardless of the techniques that you use to promote yourself, you will want to focus on creating a strong brand, and in building relationships with the people within your profession and your industry. These two techniques will help you in your career and in your job searches. You will begin to develop your job search campaign by completing the five worksheets that follow this section. Upon completion of these worksheets, place them in Section Eight of your Workbook Binder.

## The Campaign Overview

As was mentioned in the previous section, the first worksheet in the job search campaign is *The Campaign Overview* (Form 8.1). It is an overview of the structure for your job search campaign. The campaign overview follows the five stages that are utilized in building a promotional campaign.

The first step used to create the campaign is for you to state the objective(s) of your campaign. One of these objectives will most likely reflect your desire to make direct contact with people at each of the institutions within your target market. Additional objectives could deal with properly branding yourself, and applying for open positions at organizations within your target market.

The next step in developing your campaign overview is for you to identify your target market. You completed this process in chapter five when you completed Form 3.2 (*Institutions Within Your Target Market*). Make a photocopy of this form (Form 3.2) and include it in your *Campaign Overview.*

The third step of the job search campaign will have you identify which promotional techniques you will use during your campaign. This will include both branding techniques and connection techniques. The fourth step of the campaign will be for you to list the type of promotional materials that you will use in the campaign. This will include the use of cover letters, your resume, references, your personal sales pitch, and any additional marketing materials that can help sell you to the people within your target market.

The final step of the campaign is for you to provide the necessary information for you to monitor and evaluate the overall campaign. You will want to monitor your campaign to make sure that you are staying on target for implementing your strategies. You will then want to monitor how effective these strategies are for each of the institutions that you are targeting. Finally, you will want to make certain that the information that you have listed in the *Institutional Summary Sheet* is up-to-date and accurate.

Begin by reviewing the campaign overview worksheet (Form 8.1) and placing it in Section Eight of your Workbook Binder. This form is an overview of the entire job search campaign.

## The Job Search Campaign
The Campaign Overview

**Directions:** Complete the five steps below to create an overview for your job search campaign. Upon completion of this worksheet, place it in Section Eight of your Workbook Binder.

**Step 1: State The Objective(s) Of The Campaign** (Form 8.2)

**Step 2: List The Colleges And Organizations Within Your Target Market** (Form 3.2)

**Step 3: Promotional Techniques You Will Use**
  a. Branding (Form 8.3)
  b. Connecting (Form 8.4)

**Step 4: Types Of Promotional Materials You Will Use** (Form 8.5)
  a. Cover Letter
  b. Resume
  c. References
  d. Personal Sales Pitch
  e. Other

**Step 5: Monitoring And Evaluating The Campaign** – Use the six items below to monitor and evaluate your job search campaign. (Form 8.5)
  a. Organization that is targeted
  b. The position that is targeted
  c. Date of contact
  d. Strategy/Technique to be used
  e. Was the strategy implemented?
  f. Outcome of the strategy/changes or adjustments needed

Form 8.1

The second worksheet (Form 8.2) is an expansion of *The Campaign Overview* and is used to build upon each step within the campaign. You will want to begin to complete this form by writing out the objective(s) of your job search campaign in step one. Continue by photo copying Form 3.2 that you completed in chapter five. It lists the organizations that are within your target market. You will want to list these organizations again on Form 8.4 when you are creating a strategy for connecting with each individual organization.

Step three on Form 8.2 will have you identify the promotional techniques that you will use for effectively branding yourself and making contact with the institutions within your target market. Step four will have you identify the types of promotional materials you will use in your search, and the fifth step will have you evaluate the effectiveness of your connection with each organization within your target market.

Complete Form 8.2 and place it in Section Eight of your Workbook Binder. This form is an expansion of the campaign overview and it begins to provide substance to your job search campaign.

# The Job Search Campaign

**Directions:** Complete the five steps below to create your job search campaign. Upon completion of this worksheet place it in Section Eight of your Workbook Binder.

**Step 1: State The Objective(s) Of The Campaign**_____

_____

_____

**Step 2: List The Colleges And Organizations That Are In Your Target Market** – Photocopy Form 3.2 and place it after Form 8.2 in your Workbook Binder.

**Step 3: Which Promotional Techniques Will You Use?** – Place a check mark next to the promotional techniques that you will use in your job search campaign. Complete Forms 8.3 and 8.4 and place them in Section Eight of your Workbook Binder.

Branding (Form 8.3):
_____Area of Specialization
_____Personal Philosophy
_____Writing
_____Publishing
_____Speaking
_____Join Associations

Connecting (Form 8.4):
_____Direct Contact
_____Networking
_____Informational Interviews
_____Mentorship
_____Answering Advertisements
_____Volunteering
_____Entry-level Position

**Step 4: Types Of Promotional Materials You Will Use –** Place a check mark next to the type of promotional materials that you will use in your job search campaign.

    \_\_\_\_Cover Letter
    \_\_\_\_Resume
    \_\_\_\_References
    \_\_\_\_Personal Sales Pitch
    \_\_\_\_Other

**Step 5: Monitor And Evaluation –** Use the six items below to monitor and evaluate each of the institutions targeted in your job search campaign. Include this information on Form 8.5 (*Institutional Summary Sheet*) for each institution that is in your target market. Place each of the Institutional Summary Sheets in Section Eight of your Workbook Binder.

- Organization that is targeted
- The position that is targeted
- Date of contact
- Strategy/Technique to be used
- Was the strategy implemented?
- Outcome of the strategy/changes or adjustments needed

Form 8.2

## Creating Your Brand

The third worksheet of your job search campaign will have you begin to create your personal brand. Your personal brand is your image and is how people perceive you. According to Montoya, "Specialization is the single most important Personal Branding strategy in your arsenal." He suggests that your specialization statement would explain (a) who you are, (b) what you do, and (c) for whom you do it.[37] Therefore, one of the best ways to create a brand is through specializing and becoming an expert in a particular segment of an industry. This could include specializing in licensing within sports marketing, in game operations within sports information, or in recruiting a certain segment of the population if you are a coach.

The branding worksheet that follows will ask you to develop a branding statement by writing a message that combines four elements – the industry in which you work, your profession, your area of specialization, and the target market that you are pursuing. The example that is listed on the worksheet is that intercollegiate athletics is the industry, sports information is the profession, and game operations is the area of specialization. The target market is college athletic departments within the state of Iowa. In combining these four elements, your branding statement could sound something like this – *To create the most professional game operations environment within college sports in the Midwest.*

How does a person become an expert in game operations, and how does a person put this expertise into practice? The first step is for you to find out what elements are involved in the best game management environments within college sports. You would want to visit some of the major NCAA Division I college sports programs during each sports season. Find out how these programs set up their press boxes at football games, their press row at basketball games, and their overall operations. Take this back to your college. You might be a Sports Information Director (SID) at a small college, or even a volunteer, but you can make your environment as "big time" as possible. Next, you will want to continue to learn and solidify your brand. You can do this by volunteering to work conference and national playoff games. Learn how the NCAA conducts a regional tournament. See their checklist for setting-up the contests, and see how they conduct their game operations. These types of opportunities will help you to network within the industry, to see how the best managers conduct their game operations, and ultimately to brand you as an expert in your area of specialization.

Your brand statement will be an internal statement that provides focus and direction for your life and career. You should not have to claim or boast that you are an expert in a particular field. Rather, through your professionalism and quality of work, your customers and colleagues will recognize you, and brand you, an expert in the field.

Once your branding statement is complete, the branding worksheet asks you to identify the associations that serve your profession. You will want to join and become an active member of these associations. In continuing to build your image and your brand, you will want to include additional items in your branding plan such as writing articles, publishing these articles, and becoming a public speaker in your area of expertise. Upon completion of your branding worksheet, insert it in Section Eight of your Workbook Binder.

## The Job Search Campaign
### Creating Your Brand

**Directions:** The purpose of this worksheet is to build your personal brand by listing your area of specialization, writing your personal brand statement, and identifying the elements that you will include in the development of your brand. Upon completion of this worksheet, insert it in Chapter Eight of your Workbook Binder.

**Area of Specialization** – In identifying your area of specialization, you will first want to identify the industry in which you want to work (e.g. Intercollegiate Athletics). List this on the appropriate line below. Follow this by identifying and listing the profession that you want to work in (e.g. Sports Information) and list below. Finally, identify and list the area in which you want to specialize within the profession (e.g. Game Operations) and list below.

Industry: <u>Intercollegiate Athletics</u>

Profession: <u>Sports Information</u>

Area of Specialization: <u>Game Operations</u>

**Target Market** – Describe the target market that you are focusing your search on: <u>College Athletic Departments in Iowa</u>

**Personal Branding Statement** – List your industry, your profession, your area of specialization, and your target market. Combine these four elements to describe your personal branding statement. This statement will describe who you are, what you do, and for whom you do it.

Industry: <u>Intercollegiate Athletics</u>

Profession: <u>Sports Information</u>

Area of Specialization: <u>Game Operations</u>

Target Market: <u>College Athletic Departments in Iowa</u>

**Personal Branding Statement:** <u>To create the most professional game operations environment within college sports in the Midwest.</u>

**Professional Association(s)** – List the association(s) that serve your industry, your profession, and your area of specialization. Below are examples from athletic administration, sports information, and game operations.

Industry Association: <u>NACDA</u>

Profession Association: <u>CoSIDA</u>

Specialization Association: <u>CoSIDA, NACMA</u>

**Items to Consider Including In Building Your Brand** – Place a check by the items that you will include in your branding plan.

_____Image
_____Writing
_____Publications
_____Public Speaking
_____Join Your Professional Association
_____Volunteer to work conference and regional championships

Form 8.3

## Connecting with Your Target Market

Making contact with people within your target market is an essential part of promoting yourself. On Form 8.4, you will list all of the organizations that are within your target market, and then you will identify how you will make contact with people within each of these organizations.

Since you know which colleges you are going to concentrate your energies on, you now must develop an organized strategy for networking into these target organizations, and to uncover current job openings within these institutions. It is best to have a strategy to network into a college rather than applying for every job opening they have. By applying for every job that comes open at an institution you will begin to get viewed in a negative light. Stay focused on the "right" job within each college, network into that college, and be ready and well connected when that "right" job does come open. As you begin to strategize about how to network into the institutions within your target market, use one or more of the connection strategies that were outlined earlier in this chapter.

The worksheet that follows, *Connecting with Your Target Market*, helps you to become organized in the connection strategies that you will use in your campaign. It first asks for you to list the institutions that are in your target market. You have already identified these institutions in chapter five and placed them in the third section of your binder. The connection worksheet then asks for you to list the types of strategy that you will use to penetrate each athletic department. Remember that you are networking to get to know people over the long haul, not just to get a job by tomorrow. A job will come out of this sooner than you might think, but if you are not focused on networking for the future you will always be starting at the beginning when applying for jobs. Upon completion of the connection worksheet, place it in Section Eight of your Workbook Binder.

## The Job Search Campaign
### Connecting with Your Target Market

**Directions:** Fill-in the information below to show which strategy you will utilize for connecting with the institutions within your target market. Start by listing the description of your target market. Next, list all of your target institutions in the left column. Finally, in the column on the right side of the form, list the strategy that you will use to make contact with each of the corresponding institutions. Use as many of these forms as necessary to cover the entire target market.

Target Market: Sports Information – Iowa    Date_____

| Institution: | Strategy: (Network into, direct contact, apply for open position): |
|---|---|
| U of Iowa | Set-up informational interview |
| ISU | Volunteer to work at games |
| Northern Iowa | Apply for Asst. SID position |
| Wartburg | Volunteer to work games |

*Continue with this type of strategy for all of the institutions within your target market.

Form 8.4

## Institutional Summary Sheet

In the previous section, you completed the connection worksheet that will be used during your job search campaign. It listed the institutions or colleges that you want to contact, and a brief strategy that you will use as a way to connect with those organizations. In this section, you will be asked to complete the *Institutional Summary Sheet*. It is designed to keep you focused and detailed on each specific college or organization within your target market. This worksheet will have you list pertinent information about the institution, which promotional strategies you will use to make contact with the organization, and a detailed list of any correspondence you have had with people within the institution. You will have a separate summary sheet for each organization within your target market.

## The Job Search Campaign
### Institutional Summary Sheet

**Directions:** For each of the colleges within your target market, establish a strategy to network your way into each institution. Complete the following information and keep an updated *Institutional Summary Sheet* in your campaign binder for each of these organizations.

**College Targeted:** __University of Iowa__ **Date:** _____

**Position You Are Seeking:** _Assistant SID_____

**Strategy:**

   **College Information:**

      Hiring Manager: _____

      Address:_____

      Telephone #:_____

       People You Know In The Company (Name and Title)_____

      _____

      Where Does The College Advertise Their Current Job Openings:__

      _NCAA News_____

**Techniques That You Have Used**
____Direct Contact
____Networking
____Informational Interviews
____Mentorship
____Answering Advertisements
____Volunteering
____Entry-level Position

**Was the Technique Successful**_____

**What Adjustments Need to Be Made**_____

_____

**Promotional Materials To Submit** (check those that apply)
____Cover Letter
____Resume
____References
____Personal Sales Pitch
____Other

**Contacting the College** (Try to contact each of your contacts every two to three months):

Who Did You Contact_____

When Did You Contact Them:
    Date: _____    Notes:_____

                                      _____

**What Job(s) Did You Apply For At The College?**

Title:_____ Date:_____

Form 8.5

## Monitoring and Evaluating Your Campaign

Now that you have identified all of the organizations and colleges within your target market, and you have determined what is the best way to make contact with people within each of these institutions, you will now need to develop a strategy for monitoring and evaluating the effectiveness of your job search campaign. It is recommended that in order to effectively monitor and evaluate your job search campaign you will want to review your strategy on a regular basis. Review the following four items as recommended below and review each institutional summary sheet every 3-4 months. Effective monitoring of these worksheets will help you to stay in control of your campaign and to operate an effective job search.

**Target Market** – Every six months you will want to review the list of institutions that are within your target market. If your search is stalled and you are not satisfied with the results, consider expanding your target market. You might want to consider expanding the types of jobs that you are pursuing. For example, if you are currently searching for a marketing director's position in Iowa, you might consider searching for other types of external positions as well. This could include fund raising positions, or positions within media relations. Also consider looking to increase the geographical location of your search (e.g. expanding to Minnesota and Illinois), the level of competition (e.g. Division III and Junior Colleges), and finally, consider seeking positions in a different area within college sports (e.g. recreational sports or a conference office). Refer to Form 3.1 in order to identify the criteria that you used to determine your current target market.

**Promotional Techniques** – Every 2-3 months you will want to evaluate the effectiveness of your promotional techniques. Are you following your branding plan? What changes do you need to make to your branding plan? Review Forms 8.2 and 8.3 to see what activities you should be involved with in forming your brand image. It is easy for a person to lose their focus and direction if they are not reviewing their plan on a consistent basis. You will also want to review Form 8.4 every 2-3 months to see if you have effectively made contact with the people who are in the organizations within your target market. If your contact has not been effective, you might consider utilizing a different strategy in order to make proper contact. This could include analyzing your promotional materials for their effectiveness, or consider making contact with a different person within the organization. Analyzing the effectiveness of your strategies within your connection plan is one of the keys to properly monitoring and evaluating your job search campaign.

**Promotional Materials** – It is important that you continue to review your cover letters, resume, reference list, personal sales pitch, and answers to potential interview questions. If you are struggling to get interviews, you will want to analyze the types of jobs that you are seeking, your cover letter, your resume, and your references. Have a friend (or a career coach) review your promotional materials. If you are getting interviews but are not securing the job you will want to review your personal sales pitch, your answers to questions, your interview skills, and your follow-up strategies. Consider visiting with a career coach to assist you with your interview skills and techniques.

**Institutional Summary Sheet** – Your Institutional Summary Sheets should be reviewed every month or two. You will want to make sure that the contact information is accurate and up-to-date. You will also want to analyze which promotional techniques you have utilized for each institution, and if the techniques were effective in helping to establish a strong connection within the institution. If they were effective in establishing a strong connection, you will want to continue to network with your contacts. If these techniques were not effective in building a strong connection, you will want to analyze your promotional techniques and materials, and make adjustments to your strategies.

## Job Search Campaign – Summary

In your workbook binder, you will have five worksheets that comprise your job search campaign. The first worksheet, *The*

*Campaign Overview,* provides an overview of the steps that you will use to provide structure to your job search campaign. The second worksheet expands upon this overview and has you identify the objectives for the campaign and the techniques you will use to promote yourself. The third worksheet, *Creating Your Brand,* will assist you in identifying the strategies and techniques that you will use in creating your personal brand.

The fourth worksheet in the job search campaign is *Connecting with Your Target Market.* This worksheet will have you list the institutions within your target market, and the strategies that you will use to make contact with the people within each of these target institutions. The fifth worksheet within your job search campaign will be the *Institutional Summary Sheet.* This worksheet will have you list pertinent information about the college, which strategies you will use to make contact with people at the institution, provide an update of who you have contacted at the organization, and when that contact was made. You will have a separate summary sheet for each of your target institutions.

Once you have completed these five worksheets, you will want to include them in Section Eight of your Workbook Binder. The final strategy for your job search campaign will be for you to effectively monitor and control your search. You can accomplish this by referring to the five strategies that were listed in the previous section.

## Action Steps

This chapter is designed to assist you in developing an organized and focused campaign for your upcoming job search. Complete the following action steps and include them in Section Eight of your Workbook Binder.

**Action Step** – Complete *The Campaign Overview* worksheet (Form 8.1) and place it as the first page in Section Eight of your Workbook Binder.

**Action Step** – Complete the five steps in Form 8.2 and place it in Section Eight of your Workbook Binder. Place special attention on completing the objectives of the search in step one.

**Action Step** – Complete the worksheet, *Creating Your Brand* (Form 8.3), and place it in Section Eight of your Workbook Binder.

**Action Step** – Complete the worksheet, *Connecting with Your Target Market* (Form 8.4), and place it as the fourth page in Section Eight of your Workbook Binder.

**Action Step** – Complete an *Institutional Summary Sheet* (Form 8.5) for each company or college that is listed in your target market. Place the individualized summary sheets behind the *Connecting with Your Target Market* worksheet in Section Eight of your Workbook Binder.

## CHAPTER 9

# Interview Like a Consultant

ate Wendleton, in her book *Interviewing and Salary Negotiation*, suggested that during an interview a person should play the role of a consultant. She asks the reader to pretend that they own a small consulting firm and that the objective of the interview is to probe and ask questions so as to better understand the problems that face the company with whom you are consulting (interviewing).[38] This strategy helps the interviewee to be engaged in the interview process and also helps them to gain valuable information that will be used later in the interview process.

In order to utilize this strategy, the interviewee first needs to convince the hiring manager that he or she has the experience and the credentials that are needed to be hired for the job. A consultant should not be hired if they are not qualified to uncover the problems that the organization is experiencing and provide the solutions to these problems. Similarly, as an interviewee, you should not be hired if you are not qualified for the job or you cannot solve the problems that the organization is experiencing.

So what does a consultant do? A consultant gathers facts, identifies an organization's strengths and weaknesses, and analyzes their problems. He or she then communicates these strengths, weaknesses, and problems to the appropriate people within the organization. The consultant then follows this up by making recommendations for solving these problems. Therefore, your role during the interview is to be prepared to discuss your qualifications (selling yourself), to provide a good impression, to ask quality questions so as to gather facts, to identify the problems that face the organization, to develop solutions to these problems, and to communicate these solutions to the search committee.

Strategies associated with these consulting techniques are expanded upon in the next section. This includes various strategies that should be used prior to the interview, during the interview, and after the interview. The chapter continues by discussing four basic types of interviews – the telephone interview, a group interview, one-on-one interviews, and an interview during a meal. Finally, the chapter concludes by identifying the most common mistakes that people make during the interview process.

## Strategies for The Interview

Weeks or months can pass from the time a job announcement is advertised to the time when a candidate is actually offered the job. During this time span, there are three very distinct and important stages to the interview process. Once the candidates begin to communicate with someone from the hiring organization, the pre-interview stage begins. This stage is where the candidates need to conduct research and prepare for the interview. This stage usually begins with the submission of a person's promotional materials and the creation of a quality cover letter.

When the candidate comes in contact with someone associated with the job search, the interview stage begins. This can include an initial conversation with the hiring manger, talking to the search committee during a telephone interview, or arriving at an airport for an on-campus interview. The interview stage continues until you have completed your interview. Once you complete the interview, you begin the post-interview stage. The post-interview stage is the time from when you conclude your interview to the time in which a candidate is hired. All three of these stages have important strategies that you should use to help you to conduct a successful interview.

## Pre-Interview Strategies

Interviewing for a job is much more than just showing up and selling yourself. There is a considerable amount of strategy that should be utilized in preparing for your job interview. Seven of these strategies are discussed below. A Pre-Interview Research form is then presented to assist you with the preparation of your interview. This research form will provide an organized structure for you to follow when gathering information about the job search, the search committee, and the organization with whom you are interviewing.

**Gather Information** – Prior to an interview, and during the interview, you will want to research and gather information about the committee and the organization. Like a consultant, you will want to try to uncover the strengths, weaknesses, and any potential issues the organization is facing. Once you have identified the issues that they are facing, develop a plan that shows the committee how you can help solve their problems. Your plan should be shared during the interview as one possible solution. Then continue to ask questions and gather more information. This information will then be used during the follow-up phase in an attempt to influence the hiring committee.

So what type of information do you need to gather and how do you present this information? You will want to research the people, the position, the organization, and the industry.

In researching the people, try to find out who is on the search committee, who are the decision makers for hiring this position, and who has influence with the decision makers. Find out how to pronounce their names. Your objective here is to familiarize yourself with the people who are doing the hiring. Study the backgrounds of each person you will meet. Know where they went to college and what they studied. Where else have they been employed and in what capacity? Do you share any common friends? This information will be invaluable as you attempt to form a connection and build a relationship. Quite often this information is on the Internet, on the college's website, and inside their publications. Try to find a picture of each person with whom you will meet. This will be helpful so that you are able to recognize them before you are officially introduced. This can be very impressive when the interviewee recognizes each person on the search committee and introduces himself or herself to the committee member (using their name) prior to being formally introduced.

As you begin to meet the people within the organization, keep in mind that everyone you meet might have influence with the hiring manager. Therefore, whether you meet a member of the search committee or a receptionist at the front desk, you will want to be polite and respectful to everyone you meet. Show them that you are friendly and would be a good fit for the organization.

You will also want to research the position, the organization, and the industry. Find out why the position is open. Where did the previous person go and why? What are the strengths and weaknesses within the department? What problems does the institution have, and how can you help solve these problems? What are the duties of the job you are interviewing for, who does the position report to, and what is the mission of the department? These are some of the types of questions you will want to investigate prior to your interview.

Continue your research by taking a close look at the overall organization and the industry. Get to know the basic facts of the college, such as enrollment, the type of institution (public or private), types of majors, conference affiliation, mascot, school colors, win-loss records, number of sports, and any information that would be helpful in getting to know the organization. Also, what are the challenges facing the organization and the industry in general?

With the age of the Internet, quite a bit of this information is readily available. Search the college's webpage for items such as facts, mission statements, bio pages, and current news. What topics have they sent out in their press releases? Do they have some of their brochures on-line such as marketing brochures or media guides? Conduct an Internet search on the organization. Check the local newspapers. Know about the leaders in the organization. Know the organization's products and services. Finally, know what challenges the institution faces, and the direction they want to move.

**Organize Your Findings** – The worksheet that follows (Form 9.1) will help you to become organized with information regarding the organization, the hiring manager, the search committee, the position, and the contact you have had with the people at the institution. This in turn will help with the organization of the group interviews. The Pre-Interview Research form can be your starting point for your consulting notes. Do some research and find out who is on the search committee, what their backgrounds are, and if you can make any connections with any of them (i.e. similar friends, from the same area, etc.).

**When to Interview** – If at all possible, try to be the last candidate to interview. This gives you an advantage over the other candidates because you will have the opportunity to leave the final impression on the committee. As time passes, people tend to forget about the previous candidates. In addition, the longer a search is drawn out, the more antsy candidates tend to get. Quite often, this in turn leads to the other candidates either withdrawing their candidacy or sometimes finding another job.

**Visit the Interview Site** – Once the interview is scheduled, if you are not completely certain as to the exact location of the interview, you should plan to drive by the location the day before your meeting. This would also pertain to interviewing in a hotel. Make sure to walk by the room where you will be interviewing ahead of time. The last thing you want is to be late to an interview because you could not find the site of your meeting. Be prepared, know where you are going – this will help to reduce your anxiety.

**Practice Your Answers** – A large part of interviewing is being able to effectively communicate the answers to the questions that are asked by the search committee. This takes practice. You would not expect an actor in a play to be smooth with their lines if they did not practice, this holds true for an interview. You need to know which questions will most likely be asked, and you need to practice your answers to these questions. Knowing your Personal Sales Pitch should assist you with many of the questions you are asked.

**Know the Job Description** – A part of knowing which questions will be asked in an interview has to do with what the people within the institution want from the position. Review the job description and know how you meet the qualifications and the duties of the position. Formulate questions based upon the job description.

**Arriving at The Interview** – First impressions are everything. If you are meeting a search committee member prior to the interview, such as being picked up at an airport, view this first meeting as the first stage of the interview. Dress appropriately for the situation and be prepared to make a good first impression.

## Pre-Interview Research Form

The *Pre-Interview Research Form* is designed to help you prepare for your interview. It provides an outline for you to follow as you research the job and the institution. As you complete the form, you will want to identify the hiring manager and their contact information. You will also want to identify the members of the search committee and their work titles.

Continue to complete the research form by trying to identify who has influence with the person (or people) who is making the hiring decision. Try to uncover what issues are facing the organization or the athletic department, and identify what the strengths and weaknesses are of the organization. It is also helpful if you can find out who else is being interviewed, and when they are coming to campus for their interview. Finally, keep a detail list of the correspondence you have had with people associated with the institution and the search process. This information will help you to be organized in your interview session and in the follow-up stage that follows the interview.

## Pre-Interview Research Form

**Directions:** Complete the following information. This information will help you to prepare for your interview. List the name of the hiring manager, the members of the search committee, strategic questions about the position and the institution, and all of the correspondence you have had with people at the college.

Name of College_____ Last Updated_____

Address_____

_____

Hiring Officer_____ Title_____

Telephone Number_____

Search Committee (list members and titles)*

Name of Search Chair_____ Title_____

Name_____ Title_____

Name_____ Title_____

Name_____ Title_____

Name_____ Title_____

Who has influence with the hiring officer_____

_____

What are some of the issues facing the organization_____

_____

What are the strengths of the organization:_____

What are the weaknesses_____

Who will make the hiring decision_____

What are their concerns_____

Do you know anyone who knows people on the committee?

_____

Who else are they interviewing_____

Who have you had contact with – list any correspondence below:

| Date | Type of Correspondence | Contact Person | Notes* |
|------|------------------------|----------------|--------|
| ____ | _____ | _____ | _____ |
| ____ | _____ | _____ | _____ |
| ____ | _____ | _____ | _____ |
| ____ | _____ | _____ | _____ |

Form 9.1

## Interview Strategies

The actual interview is your time to shine. As the saying goes, you have one chance to make a first impression. Make that impression count. Be on time to the interview, look your best, and be prepared. These three suggestions not only will help with the first impression, but also with your self-confidence. It is important that you feel good about yourself during the interview.

Turn any negative self-talk into positive and self-confident talk. This can only happen when you are organized, prepared, and at your best. The following suggestions will help you in being prepared and being your best.

**Arrive 10 Minutes Early** – It would be better to arrive at the interview 20 minutes early and go over your *Interview Preparation Form*, then to arrive late. If you do arrive to the interview site more than 10 minutes early, stay in your car or somewhere at the interview site where you can review your *Interview Preparation Form*. You do not want to arrive too early and make the interviewer feel uncomfortable.

If you have not been to the interview site before, get a map or directions and plan to drive by the site the night before just so you know where you are going. If the interview is in a room at the hotel where you are staying, walk by the interview site ahead of time so you know where you are going. You do not want to be late for the interview.

**What to Wear** – Be conservative in what you wear. It is better to be overdressed than to be underdressed. Men should wear a suit and tie, or a sports coat, slacks, and a tie. The tie should also be conservative. Women should wear a suit or a blouse and slacks. If you are traveling by airplane, think about carrying your luggage on to the plane. Too many people have had to interview without having their interview clothes. Airlines are usually pretty good about not losing luggage, but do not take a chance. Also, it is wise to press your clothes the night before the interview so you are not rushed on day of the interview.

**Shine Your Shoes** – Believe it or not, shoes tell a lot about a person. Interviewers notice a person's shoes and if they are shined, or if they are scuffed and dirty. Shoes that are shined tell a person that you are professional and disciplined. Shoes that are scuffed and dirty tell a person that you are probably undisciplined.

**The Handshake** – When introducing yourself to people, standup, look them in the eyes, give a firm grip (not limp and not too hard), introduce yourself, and repeat their name. If you know their name prior to the introduction, you might want to say hello to them, using their name, just prior to being introduced to them. This can be impressive and show that you did your research. This might sound something like "Hi Joe, I'm John Smith, it's a pleasure to meet you".

**Sit Up Straight** – When seated, sit up straight, slightly lean forward, and do not cross your legs. It is okay to cross at the ankles but not the typical "relaxed" crossing. Do not wear too much jewelry, cologne/perfume, or make-up. Finally, either turn off your cell phone, or leave it behind.

**Speak Clearly** – If you find yourself getting nervous, slow down your speech and clearly enunciate your words. Try to avoid saying "uh" or "um". The more you practice your answers ahead of time, the more confident you will be and the smoother your communication will be.

**Body Language** – Your body language will tell the employer how you are feeling. If you cross your arms over your chest, it tells the employer that you are nervous and inapproachable. Hands clasped behind your head make you appear arrogant. Sit up straight, slightly lean forward, and place your arms either to your side (on the arm of the chair) or in front of you. You might want to clasp your hands and place them either on your lap or on the table. Since you are playing the role of a consultant, feel free to have a pen in your hand. This way you can write down the answers to your questions. Also, when a person slightly leans forward, this shows that you are interested in the people and in what they have to say.

**What to Bring With You** – You should always bring two extra copies of your resume to the interview. In addition, bring your *Interview Preparation Form*, a notebook and pen, and any work samples you want the committee to see. Some people will bring a written presentation that details their goals, their qualifications, and outlines a plan for success within the job.

**Asking Questions** - As a consultant, there will be certain questions that you need to know in order to determine the needs of the athletics department and your fit within the college. Refer to chapter seven and your *Interview Preparation Form* for questions you will want to ask. If you do not have any questions, you are not doing your job as a consultant and you are not a good fit for the position.

**Do Not Bad-Mouth a Previous Employer** – It is a small world and even a smaller profession. Never bad-mouth a former boss or colleague. If put into a bad situation and asked about your relationship with a negative former boss or colleague, resist the temptation to tell them how you really feel. Instead, turn your answer into a short but positive response. Remember to use your personal sales pitch. This interaction could sound like – *"So what was it like working for Mr. Smith?"* Your answer could be *"Mr. Smith gave me an opportunity to do X, Y, and Z and this has provided me with (use the skills section of your pitch)".* Keep it short and do not ramble on. Quite often people make the mistake of rambling on when they are asked a difficult question

**Be Yourself** – Relax and be yourself. Part of having a quality interview is to be an actor and to really sell yourself. However, you also need to be honest and up-beat. While you need to be honest, do not be too open. Know your lines (your *Interview Preparation Form*), be positive, be honest, and do not ramble on and on. Do not try to be someone you are not. Be prepared and be yourself.

**Successfully Close the Interview** – Refer to the final section of your *Interview Preparation Form*. This will provide you will an organized and successful method for closing the interview. The *Interview Preparation Form* (Form 6.1) is outlined in chapter seven, and also in Section Six of your Workbook Binder. Successfully closing the interview is an important step that you will want to prepare and practice ahead of time.

## Post-Interview Strategies

During an interview, the interviewee is seldom actually offered the job on the spot. The job offer usually comes after the organization interviews all of the candidates and then deliberates and discusses the strengths, weaknesses, and fit of each candidate. This period of time between the interview and the committee's decision should be used in an attempt to influence the committee and the hiring manager on you and your candidacy.

Therefore, the goal of the interview is for you to sell yourself and for you to gather information about the needs of the organization. The information that you gather will be used during the follow-up segment as a way to influence the search committee. Some of the basic strategies are listed below, and will be discussed in greater detail in chapter 10.

**The Follow-up Campaign** – The follow-up campaign is a very strategic phase within the job search process. The follow-up campaign will have you use various strategies in an attempt to influence the people you met during your interview. This campaign is one of the key strategies for getting the job.

**Timing of Correspondence** – As you follow-up with thank you letters and other information, you will want to properly time your correspondence. This will be necessary to keep your name in front of the committee members while they are deliberating on whom they want to hire. If your information is too early, they might forget about you. If your information is too late they might have already offered the job to another candidate. Proper timing of correspondence is critical in the job search process.

**Outlast Your Opponents** – Colleges are notorious for long drawn out job searches. Therefore, one of the strategies for landing the job is to be patient, to be persistent, and to outlast your opponents. In many cases, after being interviewed, candidates will get antsy, lose their patience, and subsequently lose interest in the job. They may withdraw from the search or even find another job.

# Types of Interviews

There are four basic types of interviews that will be discussed in this chapter – a telephone interview, a group interview, a one-on-one interview, and an interview during a meal.

## Telephone Interview

In higher education, many of the job searches begin with a telephone interview. The search committee will narrow the candidate pool down to a workable number (usually 6-10 candidates) and they will then interview each candidate over the telephone. From there the pool is narrowed again (usually 3-5 candidates) and the finalists are selected for an on-site interview.

When preparing for a telephone interview, you need to have a copy of your resume in front of you so that you can refer to it during the conversation. You will also need to have a copy of your *Interview Preparation Form*. Usually it is best to have your phone interview in a quiet room at home. Your family or roommates need to understand the importance of this telephone call and help by keeping the environment quiet and tranquil.

Prior to the actual call (usually they will call you), place your resume and *Interview Preparation Form*, page-by-page, on a table or surface in front of you. You will want to be able to refer to various points or highlights from your resume or Interview Preparation Form. One of the main keys is to rehearse and practice answering questions from your *Interview Preparation Form*. Proper practice will lead to you being confident and this will come across clearly in your tone and your answers.

You should be dressed fairly nicely and be well groomed. This will help you in your confidence, which will come across on the telephone. The telephone interview usually takes 20-30 minutes and can last as long as 45 minutes so plan accordingly. Do not talk too fast, it is better to slow down and enunciate clearly. Follow the interview basics that were outlined earlier in the chapter.

## Group Interviews

Most on-campus interviews include both a group interview and one-on-one interview. The purpose of the group interview is usually designed to involve several people from the college and to determine the qualifications and fit of the candidate. The following suggestions should help you to be successful in your group interview.

**Shake Hands, Make Eye Contact, and Repeat Their Name** – As you enter the interview room, you will quite often meet some or all of the people who will be interviewing you. As you are introduced to them shake their hand, make eye contact and repeat their name. This will show that you are confident and will also help you to remember their name.

**Write Down Their Names and Titles** – As you sit down and are introduced to each person sitting around the table, write down their name, title, and any personal information on your notepad (or on your *Interview Preparation Form*). It will be impressive to use their names as you interact with the interview team. Remember that you should be acting as a consultant and you need to uncover information that will be used in the follow-up phase. This includes the names and titles of the people you have met.

**Make Eye Contact with And Speak to Everyone in the Room** – When someone asks you a question acknowledge them and then answer the question. As you answer the question, make eye contact with everyone in the room and address them personally. It is important to treat every member of the interview team with respect. Remember, any one of these people might be an influencer.

**Listen and Answer the Question** – Do not ramble on. Listen carefully to the question being asked, and answer that question. You may want to use one of your "Five Stories" when giving an example within the answer.

**Be Prepared** – There is no substitute for solid interview preparation. Before you go to your interview, you will want to research the job and the institution. You should know the duties associated with the job, the mission of the college, the structure of the department, how the department fits into the overall organization, and the successes and challenges facing the college and the department.

**Relax and Be Confident** – Being nervous at an interview is natural. Do your best to relax by taking a deep breath, and have meaningful conversations. Do not think that the group is judging you, instead, look at each interviewer as an individual and speak to them accordingly.

**Ask Questions** – As a consultant, be prepared to ask questions in order to gain the information you need to analyze the organization. You are interviewing them as much as they are interviewing you. You would not want to take a bad job just because it was offered to you.

**Closing** – As the interview comes to a close, use the format you outlined on your *Interview Preparation Form* to effectively conclude the interview.

## One-on-One Interviews

A one-on-one interview is usually a face-to-face meeting. This meeting can be on-campus or at a regional location, such as a hotel conference room. When meeting a person face-to-face, you need to be prepared to share your information from your *Interview Preparation Form* without having it in front of you. Therefore, you need to practice answering the questions, telling your stories, and asking your questions. Keep practicing until the answers flow naturally. The most important item to practice and memorize is your *Personal Sales Pitch*. Remember that this can be used in whole or in part to answer most questions.

## Interviews Via Computer

Having an interview on your computer with a webcam and microphone is becoming quite popular. There are several types of webcam software such as Skype, Zoom, Google Hangout, Facetime, and more. In order to have an effective computer interview, you need to concern yourself with four broad areas:

- Computer related issues
- The physical setting
- Practice and preparation
- The interview

The first thing you need to do to have an effective interview is to have the proper computer equipment and software. This includes having a relatively new computer (within the last five years) with a webcam, a microphone, and speakers. You also need access to high speed Internet and have the appropriate account so you can log into the software. You will want to sign up for the software several days in advance and practice accessing and using the software. This will help you to understand how to properly use the software and will help you to avoid computer mistakes during your interview.

A second element you will want to pay attention to is the location where you will have the interview. Will it be in your house, in an office, or somewhere else? The setting is vitally important. When setting the location and atmosphere for the interview, you should select a place where you won't be interrupted or distracted. Quite often, a home office is best because it has a professional look and feel. If added lighting is needed, you will want to set up a table lamp about four feet behind the computer. And to make sure that the setting looks professional, both the desk and surrounding background must be clutter free.

Once the computer equipment and software are coordinated, and the interview setting has been established, you will now need to practice using the computer software (i.e. Skype, Zoom, etc.) and all of the computer settings. Prior to the actual interview, you will want to practice calling and receiving computer calls, and practice answering interview questions. To make sure you look good on the video, you will want to sit back a little further from the computer and make sure that your face and shoulders appear in the video screen.

During the actual interview, a person will want to have their cell phone close by and ready in case the Internet connection is lost. Make sure you have the cell number of the interviewers in case this happens. But also make sure that your cell phone is turned off during the interview. You don't want your phone ringing during this session. Other items you will want to consider during the interview session is to have your computer plugged into an electrical outlet so the battery doesn't die, dress in a professional manner, keep other computer programs closed so the computer doesn't slow down, and as you interact with the search committee look into the camera and not at the computer screen.

As you prepare the room for your interview, you might want to display your resume, sales pitch, and the answers to interview questions behind the computer so you can glance and refer to this information without looking awkward to those who are interviewing you (similar to a television news anchor using a teleprompter).

## Interviews During a Meal

Quite often a meal is included in the interview process. While this will be much more relaxed in nature, do not let your guard down and say something that you do not want to say. Depending upon the purpose of the "meal" interview, this can be a group interview or a one-on-one interview. This can also be an on-site meal or out at a restaurant.

As you prepare for this type of interview, you will still need to dress for the interview and not be too casual. Quite often at a dinner meeting, the server will ask if you would like a cocktail. It is appropriate to order an alcoholic beverage if the host orders one. You do not want to be the only one at the table to order an alcoholic drink. If you do have a drink only have one.

Also, it is best to keep your meal simple and not order a messy dish. Do not order something too expensive, but do not be a martyr and order the least expensive menu item. Finally, if you are unsure about the proper use of table etiquette, search the

Internet for information that can quickly teach you what you need to know.

## Mistakes People Make

Interviewing for a job is both an art and a science. Interviewing is a science in that there are definite techniques that a person can use that will give them an advantage in the job search process. It is an art, however, in how you present the techniques. Together, the use of these proper techniques and how you execute these techniques will determine the successfulness of your interview. The following list outlines several types of mistakes that people make during the interview process.

**Lack of Research** – There is no excuse for not being prepared. However, quite often people will apply for jobs without doing the proper research. Do you meet the minimum qualifications? Would you be a good fit for the institution? What do you know about the position or the institution? Do your research prior to applying for the job, and definitely prior to going on an interview.

**Not Practicing Your Answers** – It is vitally important to practice answering the questions that you will most likely be asked during your interview. The first step in this process is for you to complete the *Interview Preparation Form*. You need to practice answering questions, telling stories, asking questions, and closing the interview. You should practice reciting your *Personal Sales Pitch* until it becomes second nature. Practice is the key to performance.

**Not Developing the Interview Preparation Form** – In preparing yourself for the interview, it is important for you to complete the *Interview Preparation Form*. This will help you to be prepared, and will more likely help you to ace your interview.

**Talking Too Much** – When people get nervous, they tend to talk too much. By talking too much, a candidate is quite likely to talk their way out of the job. Again, practicing your answers will assist you with what to say. While you do not want to talk too much, you also do not want to talk too little. Strike a balance. Listen to the question, and answer what was asked. Reciting your *Personal Sales Pitch* will help you to answer many of the questions that are asked. Do not expand upon your statement after you have recited your pitch.

**Not Listening** – All too often, a candidate will not stop talking. They go on and on with their answer. As a consultant, it is important to listen to what is being said. Ask the right questions and listen to what the committee's wants and needs are. How can you provide them with what they want and what they need? This is a key aspect to getting the job.

**Being Too Passive** – While it is important not to talk too much during the interview, it is even more important not to be too passive. Remember that you are at the interview to sell yourself and to show the search committee how you meet their needs.

**Not Asking Questions** – Not asking questions during an interview is a sure sign that you did not do your homework. How can you tell if the job is right for you? How can you find out what the needs are of the organization and how you can fill those needs? Do your research, prepare appropriately, and ask questions.

**Not Answering the Question That Was Asked** – Quite often a question is asked in the interview and the candidate goes off in a different direction with their answer. Listen carefully to what is being asked, and answer the question that was asked. In a group interview, feel free to write down on your note pad what the question was. If the question is an illegal question, or makes you feel uncomfortable, briefly answer the question and then turn to your sales pitch. If the question is long and you are unsure if your answer completely addressed the question, ask them. This could sound something like "does this answer your question?"

**Asking About the Salary Too Soon** – If you have done the proper research, you will know approximately what the position will pay.  Typically, an institution will pay the market rate for a particular position.  If you are concerned about the salary, do your research and find out approximately what the salary will be.  If you ask the hiring manager about the salary during your interview, the hiring manager might think that you are more concerned with the paycheck than the job.  Wait until the job is offered to you.  From a negotiation perspective, they have just committed to you by offering you the job; use this to negotiate the proper salary.

**Not Thinking Like a Consultant** – A consultant asks probing questions, analyzes the organization, and makes recommendations.  As an interviewee, you should be utilizing this approach for two reasons: (a) so that you can determine if the position is a good fit for you, and (b) so that you have the proper information to use in influencing the committee members during your follow-up segment.

**Not Seeing the Interview as the Beginning of the Process** – Too many people are anxious about the job interview and they try to get an offer in the initial interview.  However, the interview process takes time.  The longer the process drags on into a second or third interview, the greater your chances are of getting the job.

**Trying to Close Too Soon** – This is similar to the mistake listed above.  Let the process take its course.  You will want to analyze the organization and properly follow-up, but do not eliminate yourself from consideration by rushing the process.  Instead, continue to collect information and to follow-up.

**Not Properly Following-up** – If an applicant does not properly follow-up after the interview, the chances are reduced that they will get the job.  The other applicants have gathered information and are attempting to influence the hiring manager.  Following up is the key to getting the job.  Gather information during the interview, and use this information to influence the committee members and the hiring manager.

**Not Being Organized in The Search Status** – Keep an on-going list of the organizations where you have applied for a job. If you are in an aggressive search, you will apply for several positions. When a representative from an organization calls you for an interview, you need to know what position you applied for, and when you applied for the position. Use the *Search Status Form* in chapter 10 to provide the organization for your search.

**Using the Wrong References** – You only want to provide references who will provide you with an outstanding recommendation. Some people believe that they must list their current or former boss. This is not accurate. If your current or former boss will provide you with a positive recommendation, then list them. If you believe that they will not provide a positive recommendation, do not list them. You cannot afford to have any negativity surrounding your application.

## Action Step

This chapter is designed to help you get organized and prepared for the actual interview. Complete the following action step and include it in Section Nine of your Workbook Binder.

**Action Step** – Complete the *Pre-Interview Research Form* (Form 9.1) and place it in Section Nine of your Workbook Binder.

## CHAPTER 10

# Strategic Follow-up

The purpose for following-up with the hiring manager and the search committee after the interview is more than just to thank the people who interviewed you. Following up after an interview is also an opportunity for you to attempt to influence the decision of those doing the hiring. This is an extremely important part of the job search process and one that is often overlooked. Throughout this chapter you will be provided with suggestions and strategies that you can use as a follow-up to your interview in an attempt to influence the decision of those people who are making the hire.

## Follow-up Process

In the previous chapter, you were asked to conduct your interview as if you were a consultant. You were asked to probe and ask questions so as to better understand the problems that face the organization where you are interviewing. You were asked to gather facts, identify the strengths and weaknesses of the organization, and to analyze their problems. This information will now be utilized during the follow-up stage of the job search process

During the follow-up phase of the job search process, you will want to know what concerns each committee member had regarding your candidacy. You will also want to know what issues each committee member perceived were facing the department. This information will now be used as you address each concern or issue that was communicated by the various committee members. As you write a "thank you" letter to each person that you met during your interview, you will want to tailor your letter to them personally and address any issues or concerns they might have. Use the follow-up strategies outlined in this chapter and the *Follow-up Mini-Campaign* worksheet to develop a comprehensive and creative strategy to the follow-up phase of the process.

# Follow-up Strategies

There are several strategies that you can utilize to follow-up after your interview. The key to an effective follow-up campaign is to develop a strategic plan for influencing the people who will be making the hiring decisions. Below are some of the suggestions and strategies that you can use as a part of your strategic plan to the follow-up process.

## Develop a Mini-Campaign

In order to develop a strategic follow-up, use the *Follow-up Mini-Campaign Worksheet* to assist you with this important process. The mini-campaign should help you to think creatively and strategically about how best to follow-up with the hiring manager and others of influence.

**Letters** – You will always want to send a thank you letter to the people with whom you met during your interview. This is the most basic element of the mini-campaign. In addition to thanking the committee members, the purpose of this correspondence is to influence their hiring decision and to keep your name in front of them. You will need to follow-up with each person with whom you interviewed. Tailor your letter to them personally and address any issues or reservations they might have with your candidacy. Let them know that you want the job, and let them know why you believe you are the right fit for the position.

**E-mail** – An e-mail message can be used in the mini-campaign instead of a letter when a decision on the position is going to happen quickly and a letter would not arrive in time. In this situation send a personalized e-mail to the people you visited with during your interview. The e-mail should not be used when a letter can be utilized. For example, if the hiring decision is going to be made within a day or two, it is best to send an e-mail. However, if the hiring decision is going to be made during the following week, a letter should be sent. Do not send an e-mail just because it is easier for you. This process is not about taking the easy way out, it is about influencing the hiring committee.

**Telephone Calls** – Telephone calls can be an essential part of the follow-up mini-campaign. The telephone can be used in two ways: by you to build your relationship with the hiring manager, or by a colleague in an attempt to influence the decision of the hiring manager. A telephone call should not take the place of a follow-up letter, but it can be used to enhance the relationship building process with the hiring manager, and to influence his or her hiring decision.

**Work Samples** – If you were going to share some of your work samples with the committee it probably should be done during your interview so that you can properly introduce the samples. However, if the committee or the hiring manager has questions about the quality of your work, it is a good idea to provide these materials as a follow-up. This can be a very natural way to continue having conversations, and building relationships, with the people at the organization where you had interviewed.

**Proposal** – Like with work samples, a presentation should be presented during the interview. However, after you have interviewed, if there are questions about your qualifications and experience, a "consultant's" report might help to influence the hiring committee. This should not actually be titled a consultant's report since you are not hired as a consultant. It is just the way of thinking about the process. You have analyzed the organization's strengths and weaknesses, and now you are proposing strategies to solve their problems. This could include creating a marketing plan if you are interviewing for a marketing position, or developing a fund raising proposal if you are interviewing for a development position. The proposal needs to be specific to the position for which you have interviewed.

## Timing of Your Correspondence

If you are the first to be interviewed, try to find out when the other candidates are being interviewed. You will want to time your correspondence so that your name and qualifications are in front of the hiring committee while the final candidate is on campus. If this is a long period of time, your strategy might be to have multiple follow-ups. The first follow-up would be your thank you letter. A second follow-up might be to have a person of influence (or two people of influence) call the hiring manager and recommend your hire. However, if you are the last to be interviewed, you might need to send a letter as soon as you have completed the interview. One trick is to bring thank-you notes with you to the interview and write them out in the hotel room or at the airport. By mailing these notes from the same town, these notes will be delivered within a day or two. Remember to thank each committee member and to address any concerns or issues they might have. Refer to the example in case study #4 that is presented later in this chapter.

## Out-live Your Competition

Many candidates will get frustrated by the process dragging on and will drop out of the job search process. Stay focused on the job and stay positive – let the other candidates drop out of the search process. Out-live your competition and you will enhance your chances of getting the job. The following case study highlights this concept.

## Case Study #3

## Out-live Your Competition

Johnny Williams was the Athletic Director at Troy University for 11 years and in October of 2004 he took a new job as the Senior Associate Athletics Director – External Affairs at the University of Alabama. Troy University quickly formed a search committee and named Dr. Douglas C. Patterson, Senior Vice Chancellor for Administration as the chair of the search committee.

During the first week of December, the University announced that there was a strong pool of candidates for the position of Director of Athletics and that they had narrowed the pool to four finalists. These candidates would interview on campus the week of December 13-17. The first candidate to visit campus would be Chuck Beddingfield, Executive Associate Director for Athletics Development, at The Citadel. He was scheduled to visit the Troy campus on Monday December 13th. The next day, Dr. Sheahon Zenger, Associate Director of Athletics for Development at Kansas State University, was to interview. This was followed with the interview of Steve Dennis, Associate Director of Tigers Unlimited at Auburn University. His interview was set for December 15th. The final candidate was Mack Rhoades. He was the Executive Senior Associate Athletics Director at the University of Texas at El Paso. He was scheduled to be the fourth candidate to interview in four days.[39]

For some reason the search slowed after the interviews. Over a month later the El Paso Times reported on January 25, 2005, that Mack Rhoades had withdrawn his name from consideration.[40] In the article Dr. Patterson was quoted as saying "I really perceived (Rhoades) as an outstanding candidate." "But this thing has drawn on, and I can see how some people can get frustrated with it. He may have got a little dissuaded by the amount of time it took." Patterson continued by stating "they could hire one of Troy's two remaining finalists or they might consider starting the process over again."

This article points out that two of the finalists had already dropped out. Therefore, by being patient and preserving, the chances of getting the job for the two remaining candidates improved from one in four (a 25% chance) to one in two (a 50% chance). On February 4, 2005, Steve Dennis was named Director of Athletics at Troy University, nearly two months after the on-campus interviews. Time and patience assisted Dennis in his quest for the director's position.

# Follow-up Organization

As you follow-up after your interview, it is important that you are extremely organized. To assist you with your organization, there are two forms that follow. The first form is the *Follow-up Contact Sheet* (Form 10.1). It is designed to help you stay organized with whom you met with during your interview, what their position is, and what issues they have regarding you as a candidate. You should complete this form as soon as your interview is over. This way you will have the person's name, title, address, and issue or concern readily available for your follow-up correspondence.

The second form is the *Follow-up Mini-Campaign Worksheet* (Form 10.2). It is used to create a strategy on how to follow-up with each person you met with during your interview. This strategy could include, sending a letter to those who interviewed you and/or having a strategically placed telephone call made from either you or someone of influence. Finally, the campaign might have you creating a "consultant's" report. This could be a plan that addresses the needs of the organization, or a written proposal. This report or proposal could be sent to only the hiring manager or maybe to the entire search committee. Each search is different, and so too are any proposals or reports you might present. Most follow-ups will not require a report, but some might.

## Follow-up Contact Sheet

The *Follow-up Contact Sheet* (Form 10.1) is a form that is used to help the job seeker to stay organized. As you finish with the actual in person interview, you will want to complete a *Follow-up Contact Sheet* on the organization and the people that you met during the interview. The contact sheet will have you list the names of each person you met during your interview. You will then list each person's position or title. Finally, you will identify and list an issue or concern that each person has for you as a candidate, for the position with which you are applying, or for the future direction of the organization.

The *Follow-up Contact Sheet* should be completed as soon as the interview is over. Your mini-campaign and follow-up letters will be based after the information that you list on the contact sheet. Your thank you letters will be generated from the contact sheet by having each person's name, title, and address conveniently listed on the form. The letter would then be a simple process of thanking the person for their time, addressing the issue that you have listed, letting them know that you are interested in the position, and explaining why you believe that you would be a good fit for this position.

If a second interview were to take place, or someone from the organization calls you to gather more information, you will have your *Follow-up Contact Sheet* available and you can personally speak to the issues or concerns of each person on the hiring committee. The contact sheet provides you with a method to stay organized throughout the search process.

# Follow-up Contact Sheet

Name of Company___Deception Pass University_____

Street Address__210 Welts Hall_____

City/State/Zip___Oak Harbor, WA 98277_____

| Name | Position | Issue |
|---|---|---|
| Ms. Sandra Thomas<br>210 Welts Hall | Athletic Director | Fit with coaches and staff |
| Dr. Sue Quigley<br>101B Lawrence Hall | President | Fit, Dept. integrate with Institution |
| Dr. James Colgan<br>100 Lawrence Hall | Dean of Students | Fit |
| Mr. Keith Roffler<br>101 Loreen Hall | Chair of Committee | Over Qualified? |
| Ms. Margaret Roberts<br>220 Floor Howard Hall | Prof. In Psychology | Fund raising is necessary |
| Dr. Bob Olander<br>501 Lawrence Hall | FAR | Integrate with institution |
| Mr. Bill Owsley<br>607 Athletic Hall | Soccer Coach | Why leaving current job |
| Ms. Karen John<br>205A Lawrence Hall | HR Director | |
| Ms. Karolyn Smith<br>110 Athletic Hall | W. Bxb Coach | Equal allocation of resources |
| Mr. Patrick Fritz<br>207 Athletic Hall | Football Coach | Renovation of Stadium |
| Mr. Kyle Simpkins<br>207 Welts Hall | Associate AD | Too many sports to support budget |

Form 10.1

## Follow-up Mini-Campaign

The Follow-up Mini-Campaign is a method for turning the follow-up process into an organized promotional campaign. In your campaign, you will want to identify the person whom you believe will be making the hiring decision. Will the athletic director be making the decision? Will the search committee be making the decision? Will the president of the college be making the decision? Will it be a combination between all of these people?

Once you have identified who you believe will ultimately be making the hiring decision, you can attempt to "connect the dots" and try to identify someone within your network who might know the person who is making the hiring decision. These people who are within your network can then assist you by calling the person doing the hiring and trying to influence their decision through their recommendation of you as a candidate.

Within the mini-campaign you will want to list every person who you met with during your interview. You will want to transfer the information from the *Follow-up Contact Sheet* to the *Follow-up Mini-Campaign Worksheet.* You will now have the names of each person you met with, their title, and the issues or concerns they have regarding your candidacy. You will now want to identify how you will contact each person, and what message you will deliver in an attempt to influence them toward your candidacy.

At a minimum, your mini-campaign will include a follow-up letter or e-mail to everyone you spent significant time with during your interview. You will also want to identify any people that you met during your interview with whom you will want to send additional promotional items or proposals. These additional promotional items could include a follow-up telephone call from you, a telephone call from someone of influence, work samples (such as a media guide that you created), or a written proposal on how you would solve their problems. Remember that the timing of your correspondence and your follow-up promotional items are key to this process. Your campaign should continue until the organization has hired someone, or when it is clear that you are no longer being considered as a candidate. It is also important to keep in mind that if you are a final candidate for a position, that being patient and out-living your opponents are keys to being hired.

## Follow-up Mini-Campaign Worksheet

Organization_____Position_____

Who is making the decision_____

Who can influence this person_____

List each person you met with, their title, and any concerns/issues they might have with you as a candidate. Place a check mark next to the follow-up strategies that you will use for each person. Use additional pages if necessary.

1. Name_____

    Title_____

    Issues/concerns_____

Follow-up strategy:
   ___Letter addressing concerns
   ___Telephone call from you
   ___Telephone call from someone who can influence them
     (share concerns/issues with them)
   ___Proposal
   ___Other (List)_____

2. Name_____

    Title_____

    Issues/concerns_____

Follow-up strategy:
   ___Letter addressing concerns
   ___Telephone call from you
   ___Telephone call from someone who can influence them
     (share concerns/issues with them)
   ___Proposal
   ___Other (List)_____

*Continue with each person you listed on the Follow-up Contact Sheet

Form 10.2

# Follow-up Letters

You will always want to follow-up an interview with a thank you letter. If you do not send a follow-up letter, you are possibly eliminating yourself from consideration and you are definitely foregoing an opportunity to sell yourself. The purpose of the follow-up letter is not just to thank the people you met with for their time, but also to influence them.

The follow-up letter should be a part of your overall follow-up strategy and mini-campaign. Direct your letters to the people on your *Follow-up Contact Sheet.* Thank each of these people for taking the time to meet with you, and also address any concerns or issues they might have about you, or concerns they might have about the future of the organization.

One of the main keys to your follow-up strategy is to time your thank-you letters so they arrive at the appropriate time. If you are the first to interview and the process will take another couple of weeks, a letter that arrives within a day or two after your interview might become ineffective. Likewise, if you are the last to interview and the hiring officer hopes to make a decision within a day or two, a letter that arrives a week later will also be ineffective. Time your letters so they can have maximum impact. You should send a letter to everyone who you formally met with. See the case study that is presented later in this chapter entitled *Timing Your Follow-up Letters.*

The format of the letter can vary, but whatever format you choose the content should include both thanking the person and also a strategy in which to influence them. This strategy might include addressing concerns or issues, reiterating your strengths or skills, or making a point you forgot to make in your interview. Another very important message to include in the letter is to let the committee know that you want the job. This could be as simple as stating "I am very interested in this position" or "I hope we have a chance to work together in the future". Below is a sample thank you letter.

# Mark DaFort
*412 S. 2nd Street*
*Irondale, WA  98339*
*Phone (321)123-5432*
*markd@xxx.com*

January 28, 2018

Dr. Bob Olander
Faculty Athletics Representative
Deception Pass University
501 Lawrence Hall
Oak Harbor, WA  98277

Dear Dr. Olander,

Thank you for taking the time to visit with me during my interview last Friday afternoon. I truly enjoyed meeting you. I know that I would be a good fit for the athletic department at Deception Pass University. I have the qualifications and experience to lead the sports information office in a first class and professional manner.

My experience includes having worked in all aspects of sports information and media relations. Our media guides have won national awards, and I take great pride in providing the very best service to the local and national media. I am excited about this position and I hope that we have an opportunity to work together in the near future. Thanks again for taking the time to visit with me.

Sincerely,

Mark DaFort

Mark DaFort

# Case Study #4
## Timing Your Follow-up Letters

Following up properly takes a lot of time and some well thought out strategy. When I was in the process of interviewing for jobs, at one point I had three different interviews set-up over a two to three-week period. My first objective was to follow the information outlined in this book and to receive a job offer. My second objective was to receive more than one offer so I would have a choice on which job I preferred. Because there was a lag in time between the first interview and the second interview, I needed to implement different follow-up strategies that could lead to one or more offers. To obtain these objectives I would need to use two different follow-up techniques.

For the first interview, I had done my research and completed the *Interview Preparation Form*. I knew who was on the committee and what each of their backgrounds was. Most of my background research came directly from the Internet. For the first job interview, I was the first person to interview and I knew I had about a week before a decision would be made. I wanted my follow-up and influencing letters to arrive about the time the last candidate was interviewing, thus keeping my name in front of the committee. The correct timing would be to mail the letters within two days and have them arrive in five to six days after my interview.

On the way home from the interview, a second institution called and we arranged an interview that was scheduled for 10 days after my first interview. Ten days allowed plenty of time to send letters to the people at the first institution, and still have time to research the second institution. Since I wanted to send the follow-up letters within two days after the first interview, I waited until I returned home from the interview to write the letters and to mail them. This way I could type the letters and make them look professional. This strategy would allow me to properly time the letters so that they would arrive to the members of the search committee one to two days before the last person was to be interviewed for the job. I put a lot of time and energy into personally writing to the 23 people I met with. The letters were typed on nice resume paper and I personally tailored each letter so as to address any concerns they might have and I reassured them of my candidacy.

Two days after the letters arrived on campus, and a week after my interview, I was offered the job at the first institution. I asked the hiring manager if I could have a couple of days to consider the offer. This would buy enough time to interview at the second institution. The second interview lasted a day and a half. Since I was the last of four candidates to be interviewed, I knew the committee would make their decision within two to three days after my interview. This did not allow much time to send letters of influence. Therefore, I needed to use a different strategy.

During the first day of interviews at the second institution, a third institution called and wanted me to visit the day after my interview with the second institution. These two organizations were about a three-hour drive from each other. With this, I knew that I would not have time to get home and type letters on resume paper and have the letters arrive at the second institution before a hiring decision was made. Therefore, I decided to send handwritten notes to each of the people I met. I spent the first night of that second interview in my hotel room handwriting note cards to the people I met that day. This lasted late into the night because I personally tailored each note to the issues or concerns each person had. After the second day of interviews, I spent an hour or so completing my note cards. I had brought stamps with me and I mailed the notes before I left town.

I now had one offer on the table and personally written notes to the people at the second institution. Later that day I drove three hours to the location of the third institution. I interviewed the following day and after the interview, I was told that I was their leading candidate but it would be about a week before they were finished interviewing.

As I departed campus, the hiring officer from the second institution called and offered me the job. Now I had two offers and a third institution to write letters to. If I decided to wait a week to hear back from the third institution, I would be jeopardizing the first offer and maybe the second. I decided to accept the offer from the second institution and consequently not write the letters to the third institution. I used two different types of letters (a typewritten letter and a handwritten note) and both were effective. The typed letter arrived later in the week, just before the committee was to decide on who they wanted to hire, while the handwritten notes were delivered the next day, also just before a decision was being made. Which strategy is best? It depends on the timing of the decision so as to effectively influence the hiring committee. In planning for sending note cards, always bring note cards, stamps, and a nice pen, along with your *Follow-up Contact Sheet.*

## Salary Negotiation Strategies

It has always been said that it is easier to get a job when you have a job. This saying is very true and is one of the keys to negotiating your salary. You have much more leverage and negotiating power when you have a good job, and are able to walk away from the job offer. Conversely, if you are unemployed, your leverage and negotiating power is significantly less.

A second key to salary negotiation is having information. If you know what the position should pay, and what others in similar positions are being paid, you will know if the offer is above or below the industry average.

Many athletic conferences conduct an annual or bi-annual salary survey. These surveys usually show how much each coach and administrator makes. They show the salary range and the median salary for a position. Having this information is extremely important as you begin to negotiate a salary. For example, if you are being offered a head coaching position for $60,000 and the range in the conference for the same position is $40,000 - $55,000 you probably will not want to counter with an offer of $100,000. The hiring manager will most likely move on to another candidate that he/she believes the organization can afford. However, if the salary range is $60,000 to $90,000 you can probably ask for more than the lowest salary in the conference. If the hiring manager can afford more than $60,000 you will have a good chance in increasing the offer.

If you did not know the salary range, you are at a disadvantage. If you are offered $60,000 and you do not know how this amount compares to the market, you will not know if a counter offer is realistic or not. Keep in mind that sometimes a hiring manager does not have the budget to negotiate the salary. In this situation the salary is what it is and there is not any negotiation to be had.

The final key is waiting to bring up salary requirements until after the job is offered to you. Typically, an organization's salary falls into the range that is paid within the market. If you know what the market pays, you do not need to know the exact salary range until later in the process.

The reason for waiting until after the job is offered is because at this point you are negotiating from a position of strength; they have made a commitment to you. Also, if you ask for a high salary before the job is actually offered, you may have eliminated yourself from the search process.

To summarize salary negotiations, do your research and know what the market pays. If at all possible begin searching for a job when you have one. If you are unemployed, do not get discouraged; just know your limitations in negotiating your salary. Finally, wait until the job is offered and they make a commitment to hire you. You are now in a position of strength. However, do not abuse this power and demand an excessively high salary. Once the base salary is agreed upon, other forms of compensation can be negotiated. Know what types of compensation are necessary (such as health insurance) and what types are not deal breakers. Negotiations should be a win-win situation and not confrontational.

## Search Status

It is important to be organized in your search. Below is a search status form that shows what positions you have currently applied for, and what positions you are planning to submit an application. In a full-blown active search, you will want to have 20 to 50 applications active at any one time. Knowing the actual position, the closing date, and what you have submitted to the institution is almost impossible to keep track of without having a way to stay organized. The *Search Status Form* is designed to help you stay organized with where you stand on each application within your job search campaign. Looking for a job is a full-time job in itself, and being organized is a big part of being successful with your job search campaign.

# Search Status Form

Target Market: _____Intercollegiate Athletics_____

Date: _____October 25, 2017_____

## Active Applications:

| Organization | Position | Status |
|---|---|---|
| Point Park | AD | Interview 6/2 |
| Southwest State | AD | Closes 5/28/ Info Submitted |
| Wayne State | AD | Info Submitted |
| UL Monroe | AD | Closed |
| Oklahoma State | Development | Info Submitted |
| Robert Morris | Asst. AD | Info Submitted |
| George Mason | Assoc. AD | Info Submitted |
| Edmonds | AD | Info Submitted |

## Apply To:

| Closing Date | Organization | Position | Status |
|---|---|---|---|
| | Northern Colorado | AD | Made Initial Contact |
| Until Filled | St. Louis | AD | |
| 6/4 | C. Connecticut | Assoc. AD | |

Form 10.3

# Follow-up Mistakes

Following up after the interview is the key to getting the job. However, most people either do not follow-up correctly or they do not follow-up at all. The most common mistakes that are made after the interview is to send a thank-you letter that does not attempt to influence the hiring decision, getting too antsy and pulling out of the search process, or not following up at all – just waiting for the employer to call you. The five most common follow-up mistakes are discussed below.

**Thank You Letter** – Many people do not write a follow-up letter to thank the people who interviewed them. This is basically a sign that they are no longer interested in the position. However, of those who do write a follow-up letter, most of these people typically do not strategically write the letter so as to influence the reader. They are missing an opportunity to sell themselves and to show they really do want the position.

**Status Check** – A status check is when someone calls the employer to find out how the search is progressing. Too many times, people think they are following up by calling the hiring manager to find out how the search is progressing. This is a fine first step, but it is not enough. The interviewee needs to take the telephone call one step further and utilize it as an opportunity to sell himself or herself to the employer. This could include reiterating what your strengths are, how you can solve their problems, or why you would be a good fit for the organization. When making this type of follow-up call, make sure that you are prepared for what you are going to say.

**Not Following-up** – A strategic follow-up increases your chances of being offered the job. Most people do not follow-up in a strategic method. They remember how well they did in the interview and they wait for the hiring manager to call and offer them the job. What many people do not realize is that the other candidates have followed up correctly and they are the ones who are influencing the members of the search committee. To increase your chances of securing the job, you need to do an outstanding job of influencing the hiring manager.

**Not Following Up with All of The Search Committee Members** – An influential letter to the hiring manager is a great move. However, the hiring manager might be relying on feedback and input from other people who were involved in the search. This could include members of the search committee, a big booster, the conference commissioner, or other people on campus. You should always try to sell yourself in the follow-up stage in an attempt to influence the members of the search committee.

**Pulling Out of The Search** – Many people try to close the interview process too quickly and they get frustrated when the search drags on. Consequently, when they get frustrated, they tend to drop out of the process. Instead, the candidate should understand that the longer they hang in with the process, the greater their chances are of landing the job. Therefore, you need to continue to try to influence, be patient, and be excited when the process is drawn out (another round of interviews, etc.).

# Action Steps

This chapter focused on how to properly follow-up with the search committee after your interview. Remember, following-up after the interview is the key to getting the job. If two candidates are equal in the eyes of the hiring manager, the candidate who does a better job of influencing the hiring manager is usually the one who will get the job. To organize yourself and to properly follow-up after the interview, complete the following action steps and include them in Section 10 of your Workbook Binder.

**Action Step** – Complete the *Follow-up Contact Sheet* (Form 10.1) and place it in Section 10 of your Workbook Binder.

**Action Step** – Develop a campaign for following up after the interview by strategically completing the *Follow-up Mini-*

*Campaign Worksheet* (Form 10.2) and placing it in Section 10 of your Workbook Binder.

**Action Step** – List on your *Search Status Form* (Form 10.3) the positions that you have already applied for and the positions that you plan to apply for in the future. Keep this form updated and place it in Section 10 of your Workbook Binder.

**Action Step** – Write a sample follow-up letter that you can refer to and place it in Section 10 of your binder.

## CHAPTER 11

# Putting It All Together

his book is designed to be a resource for the people employed, or hoping to be employed, in the world of college sports. The world of college sports is a wide-ranging industry that includes coaches and administrators in intercollegiate athletics, recreational sports, intramural sports, and club sports. Closely related are the thousands of affiliated associations that service the colleges, sell products to the sports teams, and support the athletic programs.

Methods used for searching for jobs, and building a career in college sports, are changing. While many people still get jobs by knowing the right people, or being at the right place at the right time, times are changing and this requires a more sophisticated approached to finding a job and building a career. This sophisticated approach is an organized process that will provide you with the following:

- An Understanding of the job search process

- A method for planning your career within college sports

- A way to identify the type of job that interests you through assessing your skills and abilities

- An organized method for identifying the colleges or organizations that you would like to work for, also known as your target market

- The knowledge and examples to create outstanding promotional materials such as your cover letter, resume, and Personal Sales Pitch

- An organized method to assist you in your interview preparations

- The knowledge of which questions will be asked in the interview and how to answer them

- An understanding of how to network your way into a job

- The strategies to use in the interview process

- The basic techniques for having an effective interview

- A process for strategically following-up after the interview

## Action Steps

Throughout this book you have been asked to complete various action steps and worksheets. These action steps and worksheets have led to the completion of your job search workbook binder. This workbook binder will be the foundation for your job search process. Below is an outline of each section within the workbook and the corresponding worksheets that should be included in each of these sections.

## Section 1: Assessments

From chapter three, complete the worksheet entitled *Which Stage Are You In* (Form 1.1), and place it in the first section of your workbook binder. Next, from chapter four, complete the four self-assessments along with the *Assessment Summary Sheet* and include them in Section One of your workbook binder. These worksheets include:

- *Which Stage Are You In* (Form 1.1)
- *Sports-Related Occupational Values Assessment* (Form 1.2)
- *Skills and Traits Assessment* (Form 1.3)
- *List of Skills* (Form 1.4)
- *The Motivated Strengths and Enjoyable Activities Exercise* (Form 1.5)
- *Assessment Summary Sheet* (Form 1.6)

## Section 2: Career Planning Guide

Complete the *Career Planning Guide* (Form 2.1) from chapter five and insert it into Section Two of your workbook binder.

## Section 3: Target Market

Develop a target market of the colleges or organizations that you want to work for by completing the following forms from chapter six and placing them in Section Three in your workbook binder:

- *Establishing Your Target Market(s)* (Form 3.1)
- *Institutions Within Your Target Market* (Form 3.2)
- *Target Market Contact List* (Form 3.3)

## Section 4:  Promotional Materials

From chapter six write out your promotional materials and insert them in Section Four of your workbook binder.  These promotional materials include:

- An updated *resume*
- A sample *cover letter*
- A current *list of references*

## Section 5:  Sales Pitch

From chapter six, develop your *Personal Sales Pitch* (Form 5.1) and keep a current copy of it in Section Five of your workbook binder.

## Section 6:  Interview Preparation Form

In chapter seven you were asked to develop your *Interview Preparation Form.*  Insert a current copy of your Interview Preparation Form in Section Six in your workbook binder.

## Section 7:  Interview Questions

Chapter seven provided you with five basic types of interview questions.  Keep an updated list of potential interview questions and your corresponding answers, and place them in Section Seven of your workbook binder.

## Section 8:  Promotional Campaign

The promotional campaign for your job search was discussed in chapter nine.  Complete the following worksheets for your promotional campaign and include them in Section Eight in your workbook binder.

- *The Campaign Overview* (Forms 8.1 and 8.2)
- *Creating Your Brand* (Form 8.3)
- *Connecting With Your Target Market* (Form 8.4)
- *Institutional Summary Sheet* (Form 8.5)

## Section 9: Interviewing Basics

Complete the *Pre-Interview Research Form* (Form 9.1) from chapter nine and place it in Section Nine of your workbook binder.

## Section 10: Strategic Follow-up

Chapter 10 discussed the importance of a strategic follow-up after your interview. Complete the worksheets from chapter 10 and include them in Section 10 of your workbook binder. These worksheets include:

- *Follow-up Contact Sheet* (Form 10.1)
- *Follow-up Mini-Campaign* Worksheet (Form 10.2)
- *Search Status Form* (Form 10.3)

# *Notes*

## Chapter 1

[1]Compliance Corner, 7.24.2014 Ed Column – Responsibilities of non-coaching staff members and managers http://compliance.pac-12.org/legislative-updates/7-24-2014-ed-column-responsibilities-of-non-coaching-staff-members-and-managers/

[2]Position Announcement, Women's Basketball – Director of Operations and Coaching Assistant, https://www.csub.edu/facultyaffairs/_files/WBB-Director-Operations-2016.pdf

[3]University of Oregon, "Club Sports," http://clubsports.uoregon.edu/ (accessed December 17, 2017).

[4]Campus Recreation Department, "Staff Directory" University of Arizona, https://rec.arizona.edu/about/staff (accessed December 17, 2017).

[5]Wheaton College, "Staff Directory" http://athletics.wheaton.edu/staff.aspx?tab=staffdirectory (accessed December 17, 2017).

[6]NCAA Member Schools, http://www.ncaa.org (accessed December 17, 2017)

[7]NAIA Schools, http://www.naia.org (accessed December 17, 2017).

[8]NJCAA, Colleges, http://www.njcaa.org (accessed December 17, 2017).

[9]California Community Colleges Commission on Athletics, http://www.cccaasports.org/landing/index (accessed December 17, 2017).

[10]Northwest Athletic Association of Community Colleges, http://www.nwaacc.org/memberSchools.php (accessed December 17, 2017).

## Chapter 4

[11]University of Minnesota Career Services, "Work-Related Values Assessment," University of Minnesota,

http://www.cehd.umn.edu/etcs/career/ValuesSelfAssessment.pdf (accessed March 6, 2009)

[12]Carole Martin, "Assessing Your Skills: What Makes You Different from All the Others?" SimplySearch4It Articles, http://www.simplysearch4it.com/author-articles/1303/1.html (accessed September 13, 2009).

[13]Lawrence K. Jones, "The Foundation Skills, Job Skills All Workers Need" The Career Key. http://www.careerkey.org/asp/career_development/foundation_skills.ht ml (accessed November 23, 2008).

[14]Bernard Haldane, *Career Satisfaction and Success,* (Indianapolis: Jist Works, Inc., 1996), 30.

[15]Bernard Haldane, *Career Satisfaction and Success,* (Indianapolis: Jist Works, Inc., 1996), 56.

[16]Kate Wendleton, *Targeting The Job You Want,* (New York: Five O'Clock Books) 48.

[17]Kate Wendleton, *Targeting The Job You Want,* (New York: Five O'Clock Books) 48.

[18]Keirsey's Four Temperaments. "Overview of Keirsey's Four Temperaments," Keirsey.com, http://www.keirsey.com/handler.aspx?s=keirsey&f=fourtemps&tab=1& c=overview (accessed November 23, 2009).

[19]The Myers & Briggs Foundation, "MBTI Basics", http://www.myersbriggs.org/my-mbti-personality-type/mbti-basics/ (accessed November 23, 2008).

[20]HumanMetrics, "Jung Typology Test," http://www.humanmetrics.com/cgi-win/JTypes1.htm (accessed November 23, 2008).

## Chapter 6

[21]Miguel Forte, *How an applicant tracking system (ATS) reads a resume.,* https://resources.workable.com/blog/how-ATS-reads-resumes

## Chapter 7

[22]Arlene S Hirsch, "Ace Behavioral Interviews By Telling Powerful Stories," The Wall Street Journal, http://www.careerjournal.com (accessed February 1, 2005).

[23]Equal Employment Opportunities Commission, "Discriminatory Practices," http://www.eeoc.gov/abouteeo/overview_practices.html (accessed December 27, 2008).

## Chapter 8

[24]Biz/ed, "Developing a Promotional Campaign," http://www.bized.co.uk/educators/16-19/business/marketing/lesson/campaign.htm (accessed April 5, 2009)

[25]Homewood Geography Department, "What is a Promotional Campaign?," www.geographyhomewoor.wordpress.com/leisure-and-tourism/marketing-task-d/ (accessed April 5, 2009).

[26]Homewood Geography Department, "There are 5 stages of a Promotional Campaign?," www.geographyhomewoor.wordpress.com/leisure-and-tourism/marketing-task-d/ (accessed April 5, 2009).

[27]Definition of Brand, American Marketing Association, http://www.marketingpower.com/_layouts/Dictionary.aspx?dLetter=B (accessed April 16, 2009).

[28]J. J. Brakus, B. H. Schmitt, & L. Zarantonello, "Brand Experience: What Is It? How Is It Measured: Does It Affect Loyalty?" Journal of Marketing, Vol. 73, 3.

[29]Definition of Brand Image, American Marketing Association, http://www.marketingpower.com/_layouts/Dictionary.aspx?dLetter=B (accessed April 16, 2009).

[30]Peter Montoya The Brand Called You (New York: McGraw-Hill, 2009), 49.

[31]Keith Ferrazzi, "5 Steps to get people to know your expertise," http://www.rediff.com/cms/print.jsp?docpath=..money/2006/nov/o1expert.htm (accessed April 17, 2009).

236

[32]Kris Plantrich, "Did you know? – 10 effective job search tips," http://www.streetdirectory.com/travel_guide/print_article.php?articleId =189704 (accessed May 3, 2009).

[33]Texas Workforce, "Job Hunter's Guide: Step Three Search – Connecting," http://www.twc.state.tx.us/news/tjhg/s3connect.html (accessed May 3, 2009).

[34]MIT Careers Office, "Networking 101," http://web.mit.edu/career/www/workshops/networking/whatis.html (accessed September 13, 2009).

[35]The Riley Guide, "Networking & Your Job Search," http://www.rileyguide.com/network.html (accessed May 14, 2009).

[36]Jennifer Lee, "Jaime Pollard," Street & Smith's Sports Business Journal. http://www.sportsbusinessjournal.com/index.cfm? fuseaction=page.feature&featureId=713 (accessed May 27, 2009).

[37]Kris Plantrich, "Did you know? – 10 effective job search tips," http://www.streetdirectory.com/travel_guide/print_article.php?articleId =189704 (accessed May 3, 2009).

[38]Peter Montoya *The Brand Called You* (New York: McGraw-Hill, 2009), 61.

## Chapter 9

[39]Kate Wendleton, *Interviewing and Salary Negotiation* (Franklin Lakes, NJ: Career Press, 1999), 57.

## Chapter 10

[40]The Troy Messenger, "Troy's search for AD narrows," December 7, 2004.

[41]Darren Hunt, "Associate AD will remain at UTEP," El Paso Times, January 25, 2005.

# Index

# About the Author

Dr. Howard Gauthier is a professor in Athletic Administration at Idaho State University where he teaches leadership and administration at the graduate level. He is the recipient of the 2016 Faculty Excellence Award. Gauthier has over 25 years of experience as a coach and an administrator in intercollegiate athletics. His education includes a B.A. in Finance from Washington State University, an M.S. in Sports Administration from St. Thomas University in Miami Florida, and a Ph.D. in Education (concentration in Sports Management) from Southern Illinois University.

Dr. Gauthier began his college sports career as a student-athlete in men's basketball. He began his coaching career in 1985 when he became a graduate assistant coach at Southern Illinois University. Upon graduation, he became an assistant coach at Roanoke College and then at Whitworth University. He became the Head Men's Basketball Coach at Eastern Oregon University in 1990 and led them to their best season in 23 years. He was also the Head Men's Basketball Coach at Wartburg College.

Dr. Gauthier moved into athletic administration in 1996 when he accepted the Athletic Director's position at Briar Cliff University. After two years, he was hired as the Director of Athletics Development at Idaho State University (NCAA Division I). A year later he was promoted to Athletic Director. During his five years as athletic director, ISU won conference championships in football, women's basketball, women's soccer (three times), and track. He was responsible for increasing their external revenues by 41%, increasing the booster club from 708 members to 1389, building new or renovating facilities for 13 of their 15 sports teams, and balancing the department's budget all five years. Finally, during his time as athletic director, ISU was fourth in the nation in graduation rates in NCAA Division IAA (graduation rate of the student-athletes above those of the student body). Dr. Gauthier has also been the athletic director at Southwest Minnesota State University and California State University at Monterey Bay.